Different Times:

Growing Up in Post-War England

Different Times:

Growing Up in Post-War England

James Walvin

A CIP catalogue record for this book is available from the British Library.

ISBN 978-0-9930748-0-6

Book layout and cover design by Clare Brayshaw
Cover picture of Failworth's industrial landscape, c.1950,
courtesy of Oldham Archives.

Prepared and printed by:
York Publishing Services Ltd
64 Hallfield Road
Layerthorpe
York YO31 7ZQ

Tel: 01904 431213

Website: www.yps-publishing.co.uk

Contents

Acknowledgements

This book is unlike any other book I have written and I could not have written it without the help, criticism and corrections of my two brothers, Alan Walvin and Ian Walvin. I hope they will see that it is as much their book as mine. My cousin Ada Rushworth was also very helpful: she read an initial draft and corrected errors and pointed out omissions. I owe an enormous debt to Professor Steve Fenton who read the draft with a sharp critical eye and a personal feel for the location and times I am writing about. His criticism was an invaluable mix of learning and a personal understanding. Jenny Roberts proved an exemplary copy-editor and she greatly improved the final text. Jenny Walvin offered her usual thoughtful commentary on my writing, and helped me to think more critically of my own work. More generally I have been encouraged to persist with this book by friends who, having heard me talk about the stories related here, urged me to write the book. Caryl Phillips has nagged me for years. More recently, Peter Bailey and Peter Miller made encouraging noises when I was unsure about the entire enterprise. My sons Gavin Tate and Jack Walvin have long been supporters of the project, as too, more recently, was my grandson Arran Tate. I hope they all feel that the project was worthwhile.

Finally, I dedicate the book to the loving memory of the three of them: my parents James and Emma Walvin, and Joe Eyre.

Introduction

A few weeks after I was born in 1942, my father, then aged 32, was told he had tuberculosis and that nothing could be done for him. At almost exactly the same time, his best friend from childhood, Joe Eyre, who lived across the street, disappeared into the void of military defeat in Malaya. As our father began a slow decline (he died in the early summer of 1953), Joe was plunged into years of brutal Japanese imprisonment. He was found by the Americans in August 1945, in a remote corner of northern Japan, and returned to our home town, Failsworth, a working-class community that is part of the greater Manchester industrial belt.

The nature of our father's disease, and of his protracted death, was horrifying and squalid, made worse by the cramped domestic circumstances of living in a two-up two-down: everything took place literally under our very young noses. Not surprisingly, it shaped the clearest and most vivid of childhood memories. As his health deteriorated, our father found companionship and support in the company of his old friend Joe Eyre. But so too did our embattled mother. Before and after our father's death Joe became a fixture in our home, drawn across the street not simply by loyalty to his dying friend, but also by our mother. We now know that at some point Joe fell in love with her. We also know that the son born to our mother in the last year of our father's life was Joe's child.

Like our father, Joe – 'Uncle Joe' to the children – was a deeply damaged man, but his wounds were hidden from view. He had been tortured by his Japanese captors, his health and stability wrecked by daily brutality and starvation, with fellow prisoners and close mates dying all around him. Joe was thereafter tormented by memories of his life as a POW. As he sought to settle into something like normal post-war life, Joe's traumas were so profound (and unrecognised) that he could not even discuss them with my father, his closest friend who he had known since childhood. Dad died never having heard the terrible details of Joe's war. Then, quite suddenly, in 1956, Joe began to talk about what had happened – to me, an ignorant and naïve 14 year old. Of course Joe was not alone, and running like a descant through the following account are the lives of other damaged people: men and women who were impaired by the traumas of two great wars, often in ways society failed to recognise or address.

This book is primarily an account of family life in a poor home in the post-war north of England. But if that were its main purpose, similar stories could be told by millions of other people. After all, growing up in harsh circumstances was common enough in England in the 1940s and 1950s. I know, too, that although our family life was overshadowed – shaped even – by our father's illness, our circumstances were not so dramatically different from many other people at the time. I hope, however, that what follows gives some sense of – and a feel for – the way we lived. It is an attempt to use a highly personal account to illustrate a broader story.

★ ★ ★

I spent my working life as an academic historian, teaching and writing about modern history, and my work as a historian has inevitably influenced the writing of this book. Curiously though, my first and most influential lessons about modern history came, not from books or in the classroom, but from encounters and relationships with men who had fought in the two world wars and who lived close by in Failsworth. Initially they were all reluctant to talk to me – an awkward but curious teenager – about their experiences, but eventually they spoke up, sparking what became my lifelong curiosity about history.

What distinguished my generation from those of our parents and grandparents was that we had been spared the horrible grief and anxieties of two world wars. Yet those who had undergone those terrible ordeals were the very people who raised us, and who were themselves marked, inevitably perhaps, by those wars. I first went to school when the Second World War was ending, but the consequences of that war (and of World War I) clearly lived on, sometimes in ways that were not appreciated. Uncle Joe was a perfect illustration: just one of untold legions who came home from the war harbouring hidden scars that troubled him to his dying days.

This book is about a particular time – my first 18 years, between 1942 and 1960. But it is also a story about a particular place. It is an account of life in the industrial north of England, especially the world spawned by the Lancashire cotton industry. Today that industry has long been consigned to the industrial scrapheap, of interest to historians but irrelevant to modern British life. Yet a mere half century ago, it formed a complex social and economic web of industrial activity which bound together the great cities of Liverpool and Manchester, and a mosaic of smaller textile towns scattered across the north-west of England. The cotton industry held in its gravitational pull a variety of different communities, each with its own history, industries, its own accents and rivalries, but all shared a common purpose: to transform millions of bales of imported cotton into cheap cotton goods to clothe the world. Few of us knew it at the time, but we lived in a world that was about to vanish. What I am describing, then, is a life under the shadow of the last days of cotton – the economic enterprise that had first transformed Britain into an industrial society. Once that industry expired, the communities, including the one I grew up in, began their own slow decay and transformation. What follows is a very personal attempt to describe the way we lived in very different times.

CHAPTER 1

Coming Home. Uncle Joe

Joe Eyre, my Dad's best mate from childhood, lived across the street and was a regular figure in and around the house. He casts a long shadow across this book. We called him 'Uncle Joe' though he wasn't related. He was one of those adopted uncles and aunts incorporated by many families in those days, and who were often closer, and certainly more important, than blood relatives. We had Auntie Norah next door, Uncle Fred three doors down, and they were just neighbours. For children, calling them uncle and auntie was a simple way of avoiding the delicate problem of addressing adults. It was thought impolite for children to call adults by their first names, and to call Joe Eyre 'Joe' would have been rude. Yet addressing him as 'Mr Eyre' would have sounded far too formal. Better call him Uncle Joe.

Along with dozens of other men in surrounding streets, Joe had been swept up into the military after 1939. He came home in late 1945 an emaciated sorry figure, though in some respects he was lucky: thousands of British POWs had died or been killed in Japanese captivity. I was too young to remember the homecoming, but I recall the bunting, re-installed from earlier celebrations, trailing across the street to honour his return. Joe's homecoming was not, however, what he had hoped for: not the ideal that had sustained him through the past three and a half years of Japanese brutality. Getting home itself had been a protracted business. Joe's fellow prisoners travelled home from Japan along three routes, depending on their condition. Some sailed via Australia, some to South Africa, and the others, like Joe, across the USA. As he sailed under the Golden Gate Bridge, alongside the first US POWs returning from Asia, they were greeted by a tugboat with the popular singer Dinah Shore warbling her own musical welcome.

By the time Joe reached Failsworth I reckon he had covered 12,000 miles, from a prison quarry in northern Japan to north Manchester by way of Manila, San Francisco and New York. The last long leg, across the Atlantic, was on board an almost empty *Queen Mary*, preparing to return packed with US troops heading home from Europe. But the last few miles of Joe's journey, up the Oldham Road on foot in the dead of night, must have been the strangest. He arrived home as he had travelled, kitted out in the the rag-tag uniforms of various armies handed out at various bases on his protracted journey home. The sniffy attention of British Military Police at his unorthodox military dress was quickly diverted by a wave of his pass revealing him to be 'Ex-POW, Far East'. When his mother opened the front door in the middle of the night, it wasn't the strange uniform that confused her. She simply didn't recognise the man in front of her as her only child.

Despite American medical care en route, in Manila, on board ship and in the USA, Joe arrived home from Japan a wreck of a man, though his real problems went much deeper than his damaged eyesight and skeletal frame. Joe brought home profound psychological damage incurred in Japanese captivity. These days we know about post-traumatic stress disorder and the need to treat it, but in 1945 the care given to returning POWs, and to their confused families, by the military and medical authorities was minimal and derisory. The prisoners' sufferings and needs went unrecognised and untreated, and remained a bone of contention for years. In Joe's case it was to be a full decade after the war had ended before he could begin to unburden himself about the horrors of Japanese imprisonment. Then, by a quirk of circumstance, in 1956 he chose me as his audience: a teenager, totally ill-equipped to deal with the enormity of what he recounted, week after week, over endless cups of tea, as I swotted for school examinations in his front room.

I didn't think about it as the time, but it is obvious enough today: we made a very odd couple – a gormless schoolboy and a tense and traumatised ex-POW. Curiously however, we were good for each other. In the mid-1950s Joe took a fatherly interest in me, offering a room and encouragement to study, clear of the distractions of my noisy crowded home across the street, all our sessions together lubricated with endless cups of NAAFI-style tea. In return, all I had to do was listen. I now realise that I had become Joe's Wailing Wall, a neutral figure with none of the personal and emotional baggage of his own generation, young enough to be an 'outsider' to the terrible events he talked about, but interested enough to offer a sympathetic audience, however callow and innocent. In 1956, immediately after my first schoolboy visit to France, Joe began to open up about the war and the camps. I was a curious youth, quick to bombard him with questions about his war, though there were times when I felt overwhelmed by what he told me. His accounts had a profound and lasting impact on me, and set me off to find

3

out more – about the war, and about the earlier war. In the process, I journeyed through my mid-teens believing, like Joe, that the Japanese had devils' horns.

Joe's story was, in miniature, the story of the disastrous European collapse before the Japanese onslaught across Asia. He was a dispatch rider in the Royal Signals, taking messages to front-line gunners as the British army retreated through Malaya. On his last run, the forward gunners had already been overrun, and Joe drove straight into a Japanese machine-gun post, and was shot off his motor bike. Placed under a lean-to with a dying Japanese soldier whose stomach had been shot away, Joe lay there for a day as the man's corpse began to rot before his eyes. Later, his own leg wounds untreated, he was tied to a chair and tortured.

His captors took him first to Kuala Lumpur jail, then to Changi, thence (sealed between decks in an old tub) to Formosa, and finally to the quarry prison camp in northern Japan. Each leg of the journey was marked by extreme violence. The accounts I listened to were horrific, but Joe told them calmly, in a matter-of-fact way.

What happened in those Japanese camps is well-known and indisputable today, but in the mid-1950s it was startling news – and not just to me. Bit by bit, Joe laid before me distressing accounts of random savagery and killings, of regular violence, death and suffering. Prisoners had to learn how to adapt in order to survive. They learned the virtues of silence, and of turning the other cheek. Joe spoke of the pointlessness of arguing with Japanese guards – even when they understood. The best way to survive was to do as you were told, or at least appear to do so. One confrontation had marked him physically and mentally. The guards, who had only a few words of English, liked to shout, 'Tojo number 1. George number 6'. The prisoners naturally reversed the order and the numbers, placing their monarch at the head, and the Japanese leader at the bottom: 'George number 1. Tojo number 6'. Sensibly, they kept this pearl of wisdom to themselves, but on one occasion, after a foolish argument with a guard (he never said what it was about), Joe replied openly to these taunts. The man flew into a rage, attacking Joe with his rifle butt and knocking him unconscious. Like all the others, Joe was already enfeebled and malnourished, and tormented by a list of ailments and topical diseases.

Joe didn't linger in telling this or any other story: no embellishment – merely a crisp account of what had happened, followed by a dry smoker's laugh, and a long pensive drag on his cigarette. 'George number 1. Tojo number 6'. All the British prisoners believed this to be true, of course, but it was better by far to keep it as a secret among themselves.

Joe was a calm man, not given to emotional outbursts, but occasionally he showed flashes of understandable anger about the camps. It seemed odd to me that he reserved some of his contempt for his own senior officers. At one incident at the prison quarry, a rock face was to be blasted in the presence of a party of local Japanese dignitaries. The explosion, however, went wrong, burying the party under tons of falling rocks. The prisoners secretly danced a jig of delight, after they had done the grisly work of retrieving the bodies. Their quiet glee turned to disbelief and anger when the senior British officer sent his condolences to the Japanese. The prisoners were furious. Condolences – to the people who orchestrated their daily misery, and for the death of people who tormented their every moment.

It was a story which curiously echoed the theme of the movie *Bridge on the River Kwai* (a film which Joe dismissed with a curt 'It wasn't like that'). Joe's story was real, not celluloid, and this incident stuck in his memory as a betrayal. No doubt the officer had good reasons for the gesture, hoping perhaps that his decency might yield some benefits for his men. It didn't.

Joe told this horrifying story not for effect or drama, simply dropping it into conversation in passing. It was another titbit from the war: a snapshot of wartime horrors, stowed away in the privacy of his memory, and revealed to make a simple point. It was unusual, however, because it came with a rare flash of scorn for his superiors. Most of the time Joe kept his own counsel and seemed determined to keep his feelings under control.

All this might suggest that Joe was flaunting his war before me. But that's not how it happened. He did not consciously set out to tell me about his war. It came out in dribs and drabs, always over a cup of tea, and always in an atmosphere of thick choking smoke from Joe's Senior Service cigarettes (they, not the Japanese, finally killed him). And normally because I pressed him. Once he'd started, once he'd begun to talk about the war, I was keen to hear more and would badger him: 'tell me more'. So he did.

* * *

In 1942, everyone thought that the Japanese had killed Joe. He had disappeared – missing presumed killed – along with an entire British army in the catastrophic military collapse in Malaya. The irony was that Joe had found himself in Malaya simply because of his love of motorbikes. He had been a devoted motorbike man from his youth – his favourite pre-war hobby was to ride from Failsworth to Blackpool to enjoy ballroom dancing in the Tower Ballroom. When the war came, he volunteered, asking for the Royal Signals in order to combine his passion for motorbikes with military service. His mates, waiting for their own inevitable call-up, had joked before he left for Malaya that he was off to a cushy tropical billet, while they faced an uncertain future, stuck in bombed and beleaguered Britain. The joke fell flat in the face of the Malayan defeat, and the savagery of Japanese imprisonment.

Joe had apparently vanished off the face of the earth in 1942, but his mother never lost faith that one day he would resurface. Years later she told me that she prayed every single day for his safe return. Joe was to reward her faith by refusing to leave her side in her fading years, relegating his own better interests to care for her. It was a decision that was to have major repercussions for Joe, and for my own family.

I doubt that his wife Elsie had prayed for his return. Through all my conversations with Joe she remained a shadowy figure, hinted at but rarely mentioned directly. My mother warned me not to ask about her, or even raise her name. For her, the post-war news that Joe was alive – though barely – meant something entirely different. She hadn't shared her mother-in-law's belief in Joe's survival in 1942. She had simply assumed, understandably, that he was dead, and as the war dragged on she, a young woman now on her own, found another man. I don't know who he was or what he did. But the two of them had clearly formed a steady relationship that was now thrown into confusion by news of Joe's survival and his impending return.

When I first learned about this, I was shocked by the staggering misfortune involved. But how many others, across Europe and Asia, found themselves in similar personal difficulties when the vast military machines disgorged their manpower back to civilian life in 1945? I knew only of Joe, but his was a story that spoke for legions of others.

When Joe finally came home, Elsie took in her sick and troubled husband and cared for him for a short while. Eventually she told him the truth. Perhaps Joe had guessed by then, or perhaps he had been told. She confronted him with the blunt reality: that she loved someone else, and that the other man in her life was coming to collect her to start a new life together. The two lovers set off, on yet another motorbike. Shortly after, they were both killed in a collision. Joe's first major task after coming home was to identify the mutilated remains of the wife who had just abandoned him. In time, Joe had no trouble spelling out to me the detailed horrors of the camps, but he always fell silent when he mentioned that accident. His wife and her terrible fate remained the ultimate unmentionable: one trauma too many in the litany of miseries that he revealed, bit by bit, to my teenage self, in our late evening conversations. Joe kept Elsie's ashes tucked away in his wardrobe. They were eventually to be mixed and buried with his own ashes.

I learned all this between the ages of 14 and 18 and the enormity of what had happened to Joe troubled me for years, even after I began to learn more about the cataclysmic details of that terrible war. There were times when I wept, thinking about Joe's life, and what miseries had been heaped upon such a decent man. Yet the more I learned about that war, the less extraordinary Joe's story seemed. There were, after all, millions of people across Europe and Asia whose lives were totally wrecked by the war and its after-effects. Today we know in great detail the levels of suffering – the millions killed in action and murdered by the Germans and Japanese. But in 1956 all this was news to me: a stunning revelation, one personal corner of a global conflict. Yet what *was* so special about Joe's story? True, it was a personal horror story and a tragedy, but there were plenty of those to listen to in 1945. At one level his was a simple story: the life of one man, his war and its consequences. What made it special, for me, was that it was to have a profound impact as my own life evolved. My brothers and I called him Uncle Joe, even though he wasn't a family member. Yet he might well have been – indeed perhaps he should have been. And there's the crux of the story.

★ ★ ★

Joe and our father had been close boyhood friends, just like their fathers before them. The older men had both joined up in 1914, caught up in that populist, communal surge – which today seems incomprehensible – to join the war. As they went their different military ways in 1914, each man gave the other an orange, promising to return it when they – and the oranges – came home safely after the war had been won. Both were lucky and did indeed come home four years later, and duly handed back the shrivelled pieces of orange peel which, like them, had survived the Western Front and, in my Grandfather Walvin's case, the Gallipoli disaster. Their sons grew up close friends, in terraced homes facing each other in a tight-knit working community overshadowed by the *Gladstone*, a large cotton mill which later became part of a hat manufacturing company. Joe was to spend his working life rising slowly through the ranks in the hat factory, only yards from where he lived.

Joe's house backed hard against one side of the factory, and you could set your watch by his precisely timed stride to work, the few hundred yards round the corner to the factory main gates. Like many other men who worked there, Joe was always smartly turned out in one of his immaculate Failsworth-made trilby hats. In a world of workers' flat caps, trilbies marked out the men who worked in the hat factory. Women who worked in the factory – at least those in 'the wet side', where the work was particularly onerous – stood out for a very different reason. Throughout the working day, these women pummelled and kneaded the hot clods of steaming raw felt (the basic ingredient of the hats), quickly acquiring white dimpled hands and forearms. Their hands were effectively boiled and bleached by being immersed, hour after hour, in hot water and steaming felt. On my own first day in the factory I experimented and tried to pick up a piece, but instantly had to drop it back, scalding hot, into the smelly brew of felt. Working in that room was like spending a day in a Turkish bath, the clouds of steam leaving the women's hair dank and floppy, pinned back under the headscarves they all wore in a vain effort to keep their eyes clear. Everyone agreed that the 'wet side'– dominated by rows of sweating women – offered the hardest work in the factory. Long before I took my first summer job there I had noticed its effect on the women working there: my own mother was one of them.

Thanks to Joe, I got my own first summer job in the hat factory when I was 15. I was shunted around from one casual job to another (vacuuming large stacks of half-finished cones of felt, storing and retrieving boxes of finished hats ready for dispatch), and revealing at every turn a cack-handed inability to do most practical jobs; my various bosses showed greater patience than I deserved. Gradually I got to know the factory and its workforce, most of whom were neighbours or people who lived within walking distance of the factory. Those who knew

Joe – or who thought they knew him – spoke about an utterly different person from the man I came to know. At work he had a reputation as a stickler for timing and detail, and was best known for his social distance, aloofness even, and for his brusque dismissal of people's shortcomings and failings. They also knew he had had a very bad war (though no one knew just *how* bad). Not that Joe spoke about it at work – or indeed anywhere else for that matter – except to me. People realised that it was best not to press or challenge him. Whatever Joe's faults and failings, it was widely accepted that the Japanese were to blame. When the first Japanese businessmen arrived to inspect the factory in the late 1950s, pioneers of what was to become a Japanese invasion and takeover of British businesses, Joe simply told the management that he would not be there to show them round his department. The day of the Japanese visit was his only day off work in all the time I knew him.

Joe was, of course, only one of large numbers of local men who had returned from the war in 1945. The factory, indeed the entire neighbourhood, was dotted with men back from the various theatres of the war. As I grew older and became more interested in the war (partly my emergent passion for history, partly trying to make sense of what had happened to Joe) I began to tot up the number of local men I knew personally who had their own wars to talk about, though on the whole they tended not to. My teenage curiosity prompted me to ask them direct. When I learned that someone had been in North Africa, or on convoys, I pressed on to find out more from them. Some told me what had happened to them, others brushed me off with a good-natured refusal to talk. I had had an early morning paper round from the age of 15 and the newsagent I worked for often talked in amazement about the Russians in Berlin. Another workmate had been torpedoed, aged

11

17, on his first Atlantic crossing. The postman told me stories about his sex life as the British army advanced into Germany. A neighbour, only four doors down, had been mentioned in dispatches for his war in the hellhole that was a submarine. Bill Perry, another worker in the hat factory, had been torpedoed and rescued from a sinking troopship in the Mediterranean. He described the incident to me in the most matter-of-fact fashion, as if he'd simply stepped off the sinking ship into a rescue craft. The dad of a mate from Sunday School had gone one better, torpedoed twice, in two days, on a Mediterranean convoy. One of my father's Manchester United friends had bailed out of a burning tank in North Africa. He impressed me by telling me how they fried eggs on the side of the tanks – though he didn't talk about the other kind of frying that went on inside the tanks. One of my primary school teachers (widely regarded by the class to be as mad as a hatter) had been a rear gunner, and had returned from a raid over Germany in 'cold isolation', with most of the plane shot away between him and the rest of the crew. A local window cleaner had also been captured by the Japanese and had actually seen Joe, days after capture, as they were being herded into jail in Kuala Lumpur.

I knew of others who had had an easier war: a batman who never left Devon; another, based in Dover, who cared for pigeons destined to the French underground. All these, and many more, were in addition to the older men, survivors of World War I, who, at my ever more curious prompting, revealed stories from the trenches that made my young eyes pop. And of course some of the local men who had left in 1939 never returned. One neighbour, a lonely widow, had lost her only son in the war. Now his picture, alongside one of his dead father, adorned the mantelpiece: reminders of the two lost men in her life.

There were, then, plenty of wartime nightmares to learn about in the neighbourhood. But Joe's were the only ones I became intimately entangled with. They were also the only ones that I knew of at first hand which involved the Japanese.

* * *

After the traumas of his return, Joe eventually returned to his pre-war job in the hat factory. By then, however, his best friend, my father, had been forced into premature retirement. When he was 32, a health check at the electronics factory where he worked (his pre-war job on radios became essential war work on bomb fuses) revealed what family photographs had already begun to suggest: that he was a sick man. His chubby features of the early 1930s had been reduced to a meagre shadow, and became ever more gaunt as the years passed. In the summer of 1942, when I was six months old and when Joe was already a POW, a routine examination revealed that our father had TB. He was also told that there was nothing to be done for him. No drugs existed to head off his inevitable death – by the time streptomycin became widely available in the late 1940s he was beyond help. We only remember our father as a thin man, wasting away under the corrosion of tuberculosis. To his children he was, throughout, an invalid: increasingly emaciated, progressively weakened and incapacitated. Our recollections of our life with him were all filtered through the experience of his terrible illness. His condition – his disease – was to be the dominant fact of life in our home for my first 11 years. Nor did it end there, for the shadow of his illness lived on long after his death, not merely in the tuberculin scars on his children's lungs but most vividly in childhood memories of his wretched condition and the gurgling haemorrhages of his prolonged dying.

In 1942 Dad began that classic late Victorian treatment for consumption: a regime of exposure to fresh air in a local sanatorium. It was to prove the last phase of that Victorian disease which killed one in six in the nineteenth century and which was the scourge of working-class life throughout the nineteenth and early twentieth centuries. The sanatoria isolated patients away from their families for a short while. But in time, they had to return home – along with their contagion.

What happened to our father followed the standard pattern. Diagnosis, months of isolation, followed by an enfeebled return home. There, Dad was provided with a wooden shed, constructed in the back yard between the kitchen door and the outside lavatory. It was supposed to be his isolated space and bedroom, clear of the family. It was also designed to expose him to the fresh air, though there was precious little of the latter in the Greater Manchester area in the 1940s and 1950s. Infamous for its industrial and domestic fogs and smogs, the Mancunian outdoors was somewhere to be avoided, not to be exposed to. Yet here he was, his lungs decaying, encouraged to sleep in the open Manchester air. What may have made sense in Switzerland made little sense in Manchester. I don't think he spent a single night in the shed, though it came to provide an ideal storage place for bikes, sledges and the growing confusion of household and childhood bric-a-brac. Throughout my childhood then, Dad lay, not in his open-plan shed in the back yard, but in the upstairs front bedroom. And there, as he became progressively worse, his old friend Joe was a regular visitor.

It was a matter of only a few strides across the street from Joe's house to our front door. He walked past a couple of times each day, on the way to and from work, to do the shopping for himself and his mother at the cluster of shops at the top of the street. It took no effort to pop in most days to talk to his old friend, and to watch me and my younger brother enjoying boyish things. As I grew older, I accepted Joe as part of the household fixtures. He seemed to be there many evenings, and in the last years of Dad's life, Joe would spend time upstairs at his bedside, chatting and reading to him.

I didn't question Joe's presence. After all, streams of other neighbours and relatives passed in and out, some to see Dad, others to help our beleaguered mother, all part of that unannounced ebb and flow of people which was a characteristic strength of working-class life. But through all this, two remarkable things were taking place – though they only occurred to me many years later. First, Joe simply could not talk about the war to his closest friend. As late as 1953, when Dad died, Joe had revealed very little about his time as a POW, though perhaps this was a common response among men harbouring terrible memories of the recent conflict. Years later, Joe later told me that he couldn't talk about the war because his stories seemed so extreme, so violent, so far beyond the ken of the people around him, that he feared that people wouldn't believe him. He didn't want to appear to be exaggerating. We now know he had no need to exaggerate; reciting the simple reality was more than enough. Though his wartime memories continued to trouble him, Joe clearly felt they were not for public consumption. It was not until 1956, three years after my father's death and a full decade after Joe's return, that Joe found a way of coming to terms with the war and the camps by talking to me. He had remained silent in front of his closest friend, but began to unburden himself to a 14 year old.

The other extraordinary thing that was emerging from Joe's daily visits to my father's bedside was the fact that he had fallen in love with our mother.

CHAPTER 2

Old Men and the Other War

The closer I got to Joe, and the more he revealed about his war, the more curious I became about the many other local men who had served in World War II. There were dozens of them among our neighbours and among my schoolmasters. Some still showed the tell-tale signs of prolonged soldiering, and looked like soldiers in civilian clothes. Most, however, simply wanted to cast aside wartime memories along with their uniforms. Yet there was another, declining, group of older men who also caught my eye, survivors from an earlier war which had ended 40 years before. Once a year, when World War I came vividly back to life on Armistice Day, I had a bird's eye view. As head choirboy in the parish church, I stood next to the chancel steps, and it was there, from the top step, that an old soldier called Mr Williams read the British Legion 'Ode of Remembrance' every November at the Armistice Day service. I had a natural schoolboy love for the service: the parading of regimental and British Legion flags, and the shuffling march of old men down the aisle, their chests filled with shiny medals. But it was Mr Williams's reaction that gave everything away. Anyone with eyes to see could spot the private grief he and many others were feeling.

As he did the honours, in a lilting Welsh voice, Mr Williams remained ramrod straight, looking across the packed congregation.

'They shall grow not old, as we that are left grow old:
Age shall not weary them, nor the years condemn.
At the going down of the sun and in the morning,
We will remember them.'

The last line was echoed, awkwardly, by the old men in the congregation – a chorus of aging, sometimes croaky, voices in their annual salute to dead comrades. But the real giveaway, the most revealing sight of all, came from simply watching Mr Williams, only a couple of feet away from me. As he began to speak, his eyes filled with tears. He recited Laurence Binyon's lines unflinchingly and clearly, with tears washing down his face. When he'd finished, he wiped his face and took his place back in the front pew. I glanced back to the congregation of old soldiers and their medals, and many of them (along with one old man in the choir) were dabbing their eyes.

Most of the men I knew in our neighbourhood were undemonstrative working men, accustomed to a tough, generally unrewarding, life, but here in plain view, in the parish church, I saw something utterly unusual, something I'd not seen elsewhere – grown men weeping. Seeing it for the first time was an instant revelation, a dawning that something terrible – unimaginable – had happened to these men. What could bring such normally impassive, unemotional men to public tears? The sight of old men silently weeping in public set me off in search of World War I. I began to learn about it initially, not from books or from studying, but from old men around me who'd fought in it. I wanted to know more, and the obvious place to start was Uncle Stanley.

Stanley was married to our father's elder sister, Auntie Cissie (she worked alongside my mother in the steam of the 'wet side'). They lived round the corner, immediately under the shadow of the hat factory which kept their street in almost permanent darkness. I often wondered why they lived there, not least because Stanley was rumoured to be a financially canny man with properties elsewhere in town. But they seemed happy enough where they were. Cissie had to walk a mere 10 yards to the factory gate, and Stanley, a coal man, headed off each morning to the Co-Op depot to join his delivery truck. Best of all, they were the only relatives we had – and close to hand – who had an indoor bath, and it was a special treat, in my teens, to be allowed to luxuriate in it.

Stanley was one of the many old soldiers who (like Joe) didn't go to the Armistice Day services. Their absence was a statement – along with their medals which were hidden away and never on public view. As with Joe and the recent war, Stanley was deeply reluctant to talk about his experiences in the earlier war. But I knew he had served throughout the war in the trenches, and I was curious to know more. I must have been cheeky and insensitive: an inquisitive teenager firing questions at older men about issues they were keen to forget and certainly didn't want to discuss. Still, bit by bit, I squeezed it out of Stanley. I had picked up some information from other relatives about Stanley in World War I, and it encouraged me to press on. Slowly he opened up, prompted quite unconsciously to talk about World War I when I returned, flush with schoolboy Francophile enthusiasm, from my first trip to France in 1956. I came home from France gushing about the country's beauties, about French food – and about the French. Unlike me, however, Stanley didn't like the French. Not just one or two of them, or particular individuals – *all* of them. He rebuffed my garrulous praise for France with a string of blunt dismissals:

'Dirty buggers'

'You should see the state of their lavatories.'

'Do you know they carry barrels of piss through the pub and empty it in the main street?'

And so it continued – a catalogue of 40-year-old objections to France and the French.

Even to my untutored mind, it was obvious that Stanley was talking about the devastated corner of France immediately behind the Western Front in 1914–18, and I chirpily pointed out that what he remembered wasn't *really* modern France. Even the war-ravaged region he had known had been transformed beyond recognition, But he would have none of it and he dismissed everything I said about France. In Stanley's eyes, the French remained in 1956 what they had been in 1916 – dirty buggers.

My innocent schoolboy enthusiasm for France was genuine – if naïve – and it had consequences I had not expected. It began to crack open Stanley's reluctance to talk about the war (still 'The Great War' in his parlance). In response to my enthusiasm for France, he began by uttering small nuggets of information, which simply made me eager for more, and gradually I pieced together the outlines of Stanley's war. At first sight, it seemed much like other men's war. Stanley had volunteered in 1914, at the age of 17, along with an older brother. Both survived, though both were gassed – and as a reward Stanley was later refused a pension for his emphysema because the War Office could find no record of the incident. Stanley was one of the thousands of youths who fought close to or under the permitted age limit – and survived. By the time he came home, Stanley was a 21-year-old veteran of four solid years in the trenches, broken only by one helter-skelter and ill-equipped dash to Italy, to shore up the collapsing Italian army at the Battle of Caporetto in 1917.

For all my determination to tease the story out of him, I was conscious that I should not tax him too much. The details emerged slowly, over a long period, but always, as with Uncle Joe, over cups of tea in a room wreathed with swirling cigarette smoke, Stanley's wheezing chest testimony both to his endless smoking and the German gas. We made another unusual odd couple – a taciturn older man, not given to flowing conversation, and an inquisitive teenager hanging on his every word. There were long periods of silence until I conjured up another question or observation.

Stanley's most stunning reaction was in reply to the most naïve of questions:

'Did you ever see any dead bodies?'

Stanley was a quiet, slightly dour figure, socially (and I think politically) conservative, not given to overt shows of feelings. But my question had him rocking with laughter in a way I'd never seen before. When he stopped laughing, he repeated the question:

'Did I ever see any dead bodies?'

He was clearly tickled by the sheer inanity of it. Like Mr Williams's tears on Armistice Day, his answer was a devastating revelation:

'Plenty. But what I really didn't like was the sound of rats eating them.'

He spoke simply: no emphasis or histrionics, just a cold matter-of-fact statement, leaning forward and looking me straight in the eye to make sure I'd got the point. I got it.

There was no reason to doubt the terrible truth of Stanley's story, but I suspect he told me to head off any further discussion about the war. If it was intended to appal me, it certainly worked, but my curiosity remained undimmed. Each of Stanley's later stories – all wheedled out of him by my insensitive teenage persistence – confirmed the horrors illustrated by the story about the rats. The simplest of his tales took me straight to the heart of life and death in the trenches. It was soon obvious, for instance, that Stanley and most of the men around him had not expected to survive, their pessimism reflected even in the way they ate their food. Meals from the supply lines were delivered once a day. The sensible decision, I thought, was to eat and then leave some food aside for later in the day or night. Each man opted how to pace his eating.

'So what did you decide?' I asked.

'I always ate everything at one go. If you were killed, someone else would eat your food.'

Apparently most of his comrades did the same: better to die on a full belly than leave food aside for others to gobble up. Here was another simple fact, told with no embellishment: a straightforward factual explanation which, along with the rats, took me far beyond the simple details themselves.

In the autumn of 1956, I was learning about both world wars at exactly the same time, and from two men who really didn't want to talk about it, but who had experienced the two wars at their most extreme. What shook me as much as the horror of Stanley's simple tales was the realisation that I was listening to them at roughly the same age when Stanley had been engulfed by these terrifying experiences, and others he simply did not mention. I was a schoolboy, untroubled by anything worse than belonging to a poor family. At the very age Stanley had been coping with life and death, and misery on an unimaginable scale, having to decide whether to eat all his food in case he might be killed, my main worry was finishing essays and getting to school on time. I was sometimes troubled by the noise of the family next door rowing and fighting: at the same age, Stanley listened to rats gnawing at corpses. The same age, 40 years apart, but we might have belonged to different galaxies. And Stanley was not my only unconscious tutor about World War I.

The old man in the church choir dabbing his eyes on Armistice Day was Mr Clough. We sang together on Sunday and at rehearsals. I had no need to ask Mr Clough about his World War I experiences, about why he dabbed his eyes at the Armistice service. It was manifest — audible even — in every painful breath he took. He'd been gassed in the trenches and now, 40 years on, struggled with the simple tasks of breathing and speaking. He loved music, singing in the choir, and playing the piano, even though each involved a painful, breathless struggle.

Mr Clough liked my singing voice and generously offered to give me free singing lessons, and I became a regular visitor to his house, close to my home. I took up my position, to the left of his piano in the front room, as Mr Clough put me through my choral paces. The lessons had their unavoidably bizarre side. From the first, Mr Clough impressed on me the first lesson of singing: the importance of breathing properly, of doing regular breathing exercises and of practising simple singing tasks to improve my breathing. The irony was that he could barely breathe normally. Each sentence was punctuated by a gasping wheeze. Everything he instructed me *not* to do, he did as a matter of course. He stopped in the middle of a sentence — even in the middle of a word or note — to breathe, gasping for air at every moment. It wearied him enormously. Occasionally, as he sat at the piano, he would stretch out an arm, grasp the top corner of the piano lid, and wearily drop his head onto his outstretched arm, sighing as he struggled, yet again, to get some air into his war-damaged lungs. Being in his company generated an infectious breathlessness.

For all that, I spent many hours standing beside his piano, learning how to adjust my breathing to the task of singing; warbling up and down the scales, singing 'Mini-mini-min' at each point of the scales, then back down again. Throughout, Mr Clough offered instructions in short panting bursts and wheezes, trying to grab the air, speak and occasionally sing. What for him was a mammoth painful task, for me was a simple pleasure. I think he must have been 60 years older than me, but we were divided not simply by age – he was a deeply damaged man: one of the walking wounded who could barely walk.

The Armistice service at church was conducted by the resident vicar, the Rev. Hughes – a pale old man with a sickly pallor, who was permanently edgy and unrelaxed. He talked quietly, constantly fiddling with his fingers. He too sported World War I medals on his surplice, having served his time ministering to the troops on the Western Front. Like so many others, he too remained silent about that war. When we eventually got round to talking to each other (we disagreed about the question of capital punishment) it had the effect of driving me from the church. But not a word about the war, even though I asked him directly about the medals. 'War service' was the closest I got to an answer. He too simply didn't want to talk about it.

Although I had a developing schoolboy interest in history, we received no formal instruction about the twentieth century. I had mastered the outlines of medieval land-tenure, the nature of feudal obligations and the growth of the eighteenth century empire, but the twentieth century remained off-limits. Everything I learned about my own century, and about World War I, came initially from old soldiers, though I normally followed up their leads by visits to Manchester's Central Library for the details. My real history tutors were local men who had served in that war and who had survived, some damaged, others apparently unscathed.

It took me some time to realise that there were other casualties of that war, and not always the most obvious ones. I got to know an old lady in a neighbouring street who, as she aged, was becoming progressively disabled. She was very small, incredibly pale, and walked with great difficulty. She dressed in dark clothes, and gave the appearance of being an old widow (this at a time when widowhood often involved its own distinctive clothing). I used to collect her weekly shopping – for three (old) pence a week, which was the price of a pint of milk then – and accompany her on the bus to medical appointments in Manchester. Though I find it impossible to describe exactly, she *exuded* sadness. She later told me (though this time, for a change, not prompted by my questioning) that her fiancé had been killed in the trenches, that she had never married, and she had spent her life in service, working as a maid. Now, single and immobile, she was a forlorn old lady, left behind, stranded and alone, by a war of 40 years before: one of upwards of two million British women deprived of a man by that war.

★ ★ ★

At much the same time as I was learning about Joe's war, and asking naïve questions about Stanley's time in the trenches, I was having singing lessons with Mr Clough and his gas-damaged lungs. Even then, long before I began to think seriously about the wars of the twentieth century, I came to realise that the damages from those conflicts could not be measured simply by counting names of the dead on the plentiful local war memorials. It dawned on me that I was surrounded by people who were casualties of one kind or another: men and women, some of them appearing fit and normal, but who were burdened by hidden physical and mental wartime damage. Mr Clough's lungs, Joe's suppressed stories, Stanley's ghastly memories, an old lady's loneliness – all and more were clues to a much bigger story. The devil, as they say, was in the detail.

CHAPTER 3

The World of King Cotton

Because of our father's illness, as children we spent a great deal of time with our grandparents, who were cotton workers in Oldham. Through all the time I knew them, they constantly praised the quality of the Lancashire textiles that they produced. I grew up sharing their conviction that the Lancashire cotton industry produced the world's best textiles, and would continue its global domination and beat off all its cheap foreign rivals. They – in fact all of us – lived in a world dominated by cotton. It was everywhere and it was inescapable. Cotton was like a pervasive dandruff, dusting the clothing even of people who'd never been inside a mill, but who acquired it by rubbing shoulders with cotton workers. You could normally spot people who lived in cotton towns, because they carried these tell-tale signs, the spores of local industry, on their clothes: small flecks and slivers of cotton, picked up on crowded buses, in shopping or bus queues, from cotton workers heading to and from the mills. Mine came from travelling to and from my grandparents' home in Oldham. Removing flecks of cotton from my dark school blazer was a regular routine at the end of a week's travelling on local buses. For cotton workers, exposed to clouds of cotton dust in the mills, the consequences were much more serious, as inhaling the dust often led to chronic lung disease. Cotton killed them in their thousands.

King Cotton lay at the heart of an extraordinary regional industrial complex, and L.S. Lowry wasn't the only one struck by its industrial panorama. One of my favourite schoolboy pastimes was to count the factory chimneys that ringed the world I lived in. A short walk took me from the back of our house in Failsworth, across the fields to Woodhouses, a village at the eastern edge of the town. Halfway, from a vantage point on top of a hillock (which we unaccountably named 'Cowboy Hill'), I could watch the whole industrial process of greater Manchester at work. I would slowly rotate through 360 degrees, scanning the varied geography of the surrounding region. To the south, lay the flat lands of Manchester itself; behind me, gently rising to the north, the Pennines. What impressed me most, however, was the vast array of factory chimneys and the high-rise clutter of other industries (colliery winding gear, for instance) scattered to all points of the compass. Some of the factory chimneys were close by and massive; others, on the far horizon, little more than indistinct matchsticks. To the south-west lay the heavy industrial areas of Manchester and Salford; to the west the mills of Rochdale; then north to Oldham's cotton factories. As I turned to look east and south, via Stalybridge and Ashton, I saw more cotton mills and factories, before glancing towards Stockport, finally completing the circle by looking back again to Manchester. On working days, with factory smoke trailing skywards, it offered an extraordinary industrial landscape, though it was clearer at weekends when the factories lay silent and the chimneys smokeless. I often counted them, and though I now forget how many there were precisely, they were to be counted by the dozen, many of them with the factory name emblazoned in tiled bricks at the top of the chimney: the *Argyle, Elk, United, Regent*. My home town, indeed the entire region, seemed hemmed in by these spiky industrial monuments. It was an exact vision of this murky, chimney-dominated industrial landscape – only 20 miles to the west – that had struck George Orwell so forcibly on his first foray north 20 years before, and which became the setting for his classic *Road to Wigan Pier*.

Strictly speaking, much of the panorama I gazed at was not Manchester at all, but rather a medley of smaller towns, all held in the gravitational pull of Manchester, each with its own distinctive industry: hats in Stockport, cotton in Oldham, heavy engineering and docks in Salford. And everywhere there was a range of other industries (rubber, metal, mining, docks and railways) all supporting the dominant world of textile production. Sprawling across the entire region lay the remnants of a once massive coal industry, with pits dotting the Lancashire coalfield, and which continued to fuel the cotton and other local industries. In 1880 Lancashire boasted 534 pits. By 2007, only two survived. It had been these very coal seams which had lured the coal-mining Walvins from Derbyshire to north Manchester in the first place. Family tales of Grandpa Walvin's multiple black/blue coal dust scars all over his body first aroused my understanding about the terrible nature of coal mining.

Each of the towns whose chimneys I counted as a boy had its own identity, its own local government and industrial specialism, and all accompanied by local customs, distinct accents and dialects. Accents, and even vocabulary, seemed to change over a matter of yards: round the corner, or a mere bus stop away. Accents and intonations changed from Oldham to Manchester, from Rochdale to Bury, and everywhere in between. Sometimes it was only a matter of inflection and emphasis, or a different usage of particular words, but insiders could spot these distinctions. My grandfather Wood was Oldham to his well-worn boots, uncompromising in his Oldham accent and vocabulary. (He totally nonplussed a waitress in London – we were there for a Rugby League Final in 1957 – by asking 'Hast got a few shives of bread and butter?'.) He was born and raised as a 'thee' and 'thou' man, not like the French *tu-toi* version, but the old English version that was used whoever you were speaking to. Outsiders tended to lump us all together as 'northerners'. ('Do I hear a north countryman speaking?' asked one fashionable English lady, honking like a seal, at a fancy party in Los Angeles a lifetime later.) Locals, however, appreciated the complex distinctions among us. In their turn, these distinctions fed fierce local loyalties, best seen perhaps in sporting rivalries. The pioneering football teams and leagues of the North West (the origins of the modern professional game) grew out of these self-same local identities and rivalries. Much the same was true of Lancashire League cricket, local brass bands and rugby teams, all of them reflecting and drawing upon local – sometimes parochial – distinctions.

Despite all these local variations, and despite the industrial differences from place to place, cotton still dominated. Though I didn't know it at the time, its days were numbered. At the very moment I was turning my circle, and counting the factory chimneys around me, the hard economic evidence behind that panorama was irrefutable. In 1912 the cotton industry had employed 800,000, but between the wars it had lost the best part of 300,000 workers. World War II had given the industry a temporary boost, and even though in the mid-1950s it still employed 200,000 people, the years of my own childhood formed an era of decline and attrition for cotton. Burdened by outdated plant and labour practices, faced by fierce competition from Asia, the Lancashire cotton industry was already doomed. By 1958 Britain had become a net importer of cotton goods. Though I became aware, in my late teens, of the political battles waged unsuccessfully to protect the industry, viewed from my vantage point in Failsworth, all this seemed mere political noises offstage. Cotton was, I thought, and would remain, king.

★ ★ ★

At the heart of this sprawling, smoky region lay the city of Manchester, its recent history, fortunes and rivalries linked directly to the story of the great port of Liverpool. In the 1950s Manchester remained what it had been for a century and a half, both a manufacturing city and the focal point of a web of industries which covered the entire north west of England. Outsiders looked down on the place as a grubby provincial backwater (even Orwell thought it 'beastly'), but it was in fact the centre of an astonishing global system, and Manchester's civic pride was rooted in the city's remarkable international history and achievements. Like other great Victorian cities, Manchester proclaimed its attainments through its major civic buildings: the Town Hall, the Free Trade Hall, and those banks, libraries, galleries, museums and places of learning which dominated the heart of the city, and which lined the major streets radiating from the city centre. In the 1950s it was the northern HQ of a string of national enterprises, and boasted a string of internationally renowned institutions: a newspaper, *The Manchester Guardian* (*The Guardian* from 1959); an orchestra, the Hallé under the direction of Sir John Barbirolli; a university, the Victoria University of Manchester; a direct-grant grammar school, Manchester

Grammar School under Eric James; and Manchester United under Matt Busby. In fact modern industrial Manchester had traditionally seen itself as an international city. The city's coat of arms (granted in 1842) displayed a sailing ship which proclaimed the city's commercial and industrial links to the wider world. But the prime link was to the world of cotton. It was the first city of the Industrial Revolution and that, above all, meant cotton.

Millions of tons of imported raw cotton (80% of it from the slave plantations of the US South in 1860) were converted into millions of yards of cheap textiles which spilled out from Lancashire to clothe the world. Though long past its peak, as late as 1950 Lancashire exported 823 million yards of cotton cloths. But by then, the graph of raw cotton imports and of textile exports was ever downwards, and the writing was on the grimy industrial wall. In the nineteenth century, people had flocked to Manchester from across Europe, to work there, to invest there, and to study what was happening in the world's first industrial city. By the time I left home in 1960, a different kind of people had begun to arrive: growing numbers of people from the Indian sub-continent who came to work in the mills that locals had begun to desert in their thousands. That year, the first Asian family settled in my grandparents' street in Oldham. Today, that street is entirely Asian.

★ ★ ★

For all its self-belief and importance, there was no escaping the fact that, like other industrial cities at the time, Manchester was a dirty place. Smoke, from hundreds of factories, and from tens of thousands of coal-heated houses, had seeped into its grand Victorian heart, redecorating the entire city, and giving its red brick and white stone Victorian buildings a blackened and slightly sinister veneer. The formidable Victorian buildings I explored in my teenage years were all black: the Town Hall, the Art Gallery, the Free Trade Hall – even the Cathedral. Only those buildings opened in the twentieth century (notably the Central Library, my home-from-home by the late 1950s) seemed to have escaped the darkening process. The all-pervading grime even affected the way we all looked. Poorer then than now, people had fewer clothes and tended to opt for practical, 'sensible' clothing: anything white or pale was soon vanquished by the dirt that regularly shrouded the entire city. In a world without widespread instant hot water and modern washing facilities, washing yourself and your clothes was much less easy, and we looked – and felt – much grubbier then than now.

As a schoolboy (and I suppose like everyone else) I carried with me personal evidence of the atmospheric muck that was daily life in Manchester, in the form of my filthy shirt collars and my unspeakable handkerchief. At secondary school I wore detached collars. At first I found them uncomfortable and old-fashioned, better suited to my grandfather than to a teenager. But it was much easier and more practical to replace and wash a collar than the whole shirt. Each evening I removed a collar edged with a layer of dirt. It reminded me of the tidemark left behind in an emptying bath, itself another tell-tale sign. But the real proof of Manchester's atmosphere was to be seen in the contents of your handkerchief. You always carried a hankie, not because of a permanent cold (though we got plenty of those) but because you needed to get rid of the blackened snot and bronchial filth that accompanied local life. Most of us used a handkerchief to clear the nose, but older men, clinging to disappearing habits, still spat in public, or cleaned their nose by simply snorting out the contents in public (much as some sportsmen continue to do).

Underneath all this muck, and despite its grubby façade, Manchester was a city with serious cultural roots: its newspaper, its music and libraries, its science and learning, its sport, all managed to thrive in that sooty sprawl. Like thousands of others, as I grew up I had my own access to each. *The Manchester Guardian* became my daily guide to the world at large, especially after 1956 when I started the early morning newspaper round and had free access to all the newspapers piled in Mr Buckley's newspaper shop. The Hallé played in the Free Trade Hall, exactly half way between my school and home (and where I changed buses). The school occasionally bused us in to watch the Hallé in rehearsal. I remember Barbirolli sternly hectoring the largely indifferent schoolboys against popular musical trends. He predictably lost out to Bill Haley. The bus from school dropped me outside Manchester Central Library and, once I'd mustered up the initial courage to go through its forbidding entrance and claim a seat, it became my favourite place in the whole of Manchester (apart, that is, from Old Trafford).

The bus to and from school also went straight past the main entrance to Manchester University, and from an early age I was determined to go there, a much bolder ambition then than now as in the 1950s the great majority left school at 15 and only a tiny minority went on to higher education. In my mid-teens I even took to buying exercise books from the university bookshop, because they came embossed with the university crest and, in some indefinable way, seemed to hold out the prospect of life as a university student. In the event, at 18 I needed to be away: away from Manchester, away from home, from everything, and I headed elsewhere to study. I went south, though not too far south. When new friends asked where I came from I usually took the easy way out and said Manchester, though strictly speaking I was born and raised in Failsworth, schooled in Manchester and had spent much of my free time in Oldham. So where did my local parochial loyalties lie? It was much easier just to say I came from Manchester.

CHAPTER 4

A Death in the Family

By the end of the war, and by the time Joe Eyre had returned from Japan, my parents had two sons, myself and Alan (who had been born as if to coincide with victory in Europe). Our father had long since stopped working. After the diagnosis of TB in 1942, and his initial spell in the sanatorium, he came home to endure what became a prolonged slide towards the inevitable. Dad's illness and decline was a common and familiar story in early twentieth-century Britain. Even the mention of TB sent a communal shiver down people's spine. It had, since time out of mind, been a major scourge, a killer of all sorts and conditions of people, but was particularly ferocious in poor urban communities. It was also a disease which had long perplexed and taxed medical science, and although it had peaked in Britain in the 1860s and declined sharply from the 1930s, it continued to wreak havoc. It remained the single greatest killer of males under the age of 44 until replaced by cancer and coronary disease in the post-war years, and it killed half of all women who died before the age of 24. Medical science struggled to cope, even with the declining disease, offering a confusion of medical and social solutions, most famously the drive to isolate patients, and to expose them to fresh air. Influenced by new practices in Europe and the USA, sanatoria proliferated in twentieth-century Britain, and it was there, in those bleak unforgiving places, that TB victims were exposed, for months at a time, not merely to the vagaries of local weather (and often industrial pollution) but also to various demoralising harsh regimes of deprivation. Curiously, two of the most influential early twentieth-century pioneers in treating TB patients and their families had been the Medical Officers for Health in Oldham and Manchester, the very region we lived in.

Mass radiography, introduced during World War II, had spotted our father's condition, but mere diagnosis was only the beginning. In 1941, the year before Dad's condition was discovered, there were only 28,087 beds available for the 77,000 people suffering from infectious TB. Once a patient returned home, strict rules about the segregation of family members from the patient were supposed to apply. Sleeping, washing, cooking and eating were supposed to take place away from the patient, all designed to curb the spread of TB within the family. The real medical breakthrough, the discovery of streptomycin in 1943, and its availability from 1946, came too late to save our father. Like thousands of others, he was doomed. Thus the general hardships of the immediate post-war years – rationing, shortages and exceptionally cold weather – while bleak for everyone, seemed much worse with a fatally sick man in the house, and the grisly nature of his illness made it even harder to bear.

In a two-up two-down there was no healthy escape from the accelerating and worsening crises. The 'fresh-air shelter' in the yard was supposed to insulate the rest of us from the worst of Dad's contagion, but it proved totally impractical. His illness struck in ever more severe bouts, but there was never really a moment when he seemed normal, or moderately healthy, like other men. Even short and ever slower walks, for example the short distance to the local cinema – *Failsworth Popular Picture Palace* – left him struggling and in need of yet another rest. He wanted to go into Manchester to watch United, but the simple effort of clambering onto two buses proved too exhausting. As his condition worsened, and as his two sons grew and began to appreciate the reality of his illness, his social and physical horizons contracted. He was also aging before his time. Still in his thirties, he began to behave as old people did, getting his social life by standing for hours at the front door, his life defined and limited by what went on in the neighbouring streets, though always cheered by visits from friends – especially Joe.

Dad's illness dominated and shaped everything we did, or couldn't do. Our mother took her children for regular check-ups to a TB clinic in Oldham, and the medical staff gave her strict guidelines about the management of a TB-stricken household. Ideally, everything in the house had to be carefully demarcated and separated. Dad was supposed to have his own towels, soap and eating utensils; the rest of the family was not to touch or use anything that belonged to him. However prudent, such rules and guidelines were completely impractical in a poor crowded home; they were ideals far beyond our reach. There was not enough cutlery or crockery to provide two separate sets, one for Dad, the other for the rest of us. There were not enough towels or bedding to enable mother to distinguish and safeguard what was his and what was ours. GPs who tended stricken families recognised these problems, which were more social than medical, and a lively correspondence periodically flared in medical journals about the need to improve housing for families such as ours. In our particular case, and I am sure in common with many others, the one major problem was the household sink.

There was only one sink. We all washed in it, and scrubbed the pots and plates in it. Yet it was the same sink that Dad leaned over (or was held over) when wracked by a haemorrhage. I can't, now, recall when I first noticed these terrible outbursts of coughing and retching, which got worse as the illness took hold, but I have vivid early memories of special pots, provided by the hospital, being whisked away, covered with towels, from his bedside, and the contents either sluiced down the lavatory (at the bottom of the yard) or swilled down the sink. When dad was up and about, he was periodically and suddenly convulsed by coughing bouts, and it was then that mother – if she was at home – quickly steered him towards the sink in the kitchen. In the hurried confusion that followed, Alan and I were promptly shepherded away, out of the room, out of the house, shooed upstairs or into the front room. For our mother, all this involved a horrible but regular human juggling act – getting her husband to the sink, holding him there, and steering her children elsewhere. But there's a limit to what a harassed women can do, on her own, when faced with a feeble vomiting man and two curious small boys she wants to shield and safeguard – and all at the same time. Inevitably there were times when my brother and I saw all too clearly what was happening.

Mother was a physically strong woman, and would hold Dad securely from behind, trying to anchor him to the sink, but it was hard work even when she was handling a greatly enfeebled man. She struggled to keep him upright and focused at the sink, while ordering us elsewhere. With another adult on hand, the children could be handled easily, but on those increasing numbers of occasions when she was stranded, coping on her own, it was inevitable that we would be drawn into the squalid reality of a man gradually succumbing to TB. I suppose we were frightened by what was happening, but above all I was also curious, and wanted to see. My memory of these sessions tends to be confused, but there were spurts of blood and clots of – what? ... tissue? – swirling into the family sink. Perhaps, as I get older, these images have become more extreme, more revolting. But they were bad enough at the time.

Mum clearly needed other people to help, but people had good reason to steer clear of a house infected by TB. There was an understandable stigma, and a genuine fear, about families with TB. We were an infected – and infectious – household. Patients themselves sometimes tried to hide their illness (when looking for work, for example), and people were often reluctant to linger too long in a house stricken by TB. People were, quite simply, afraid of catching the disease. Despite all this, we were lucky: we had helpful neighbours, and local relatives who never hesitated to help, and who whisked away the children when necessary. And there was always Uncle Joe. Not only was he a regular visitor, but he was readily on hand, living only a few yards away across the road. Any personal squeamishness Joe might once have felt had long since vanished in the squalor of Japanese prison camps. He later told me how close mates had died, huddled in the straw next to him, in a bitter Japanese winter. One, a friend from Rochdale, died with his stiffened arm thrown across Joe's sleeping face. Prisoners had cared for each other, cleaning men incapacitated by dysentery as they would a soiled baby. Joe described how he had been part of a team helping to hold men down when army doctors undertook primitive surgery – without anaesthetics – in the dire conditions of the camps. (The day after the Japanese guards fled, in August 1945, the prisoners found all the medicines they needed, rotting in unopened Red Cross parcels in a locked shed.) Joe had survived the grimmest of human suffering, and had seen the most abject of human conditions. Crowded prison camps, bolted below decks in a rusting tub that transported him first to Formosa, then to Japan, and finally driven to collapse in what was effectively a slave quarry. After all that, what else was there to feel squeamish about? Handling a sick friend was not something to repel him.

We now know that there was more to Joe's visits than merely to see his old friend. At some point, and for reasons that are all too readily understood, Joe and our mother became lovers. In the confusion and the mess of Dad's decline, the two of them began an affair which was to continue for years. All this happened when I was a small boy and I knew nothing about it at the time, though the penny dropped – after a fashion – in my teens. It must, however, have been fairly obvious to other adults, relatives and neighbours – and certainly to our father. Notwithstanding Joe's long-standing friendship, his frequent presence in the house must have prompted curiosity and gossip among the locals. This was, after all, a tight community of small streets, to say nothing of twitching front room curtains. Little passed unnoticed. People clearly knew that an unusual arrangement was evolving between our parents and Dad's oldest friend.

★ ★ ★

Our father's last few weeks were spent in hospital in Oldham. By then, I realised he would not come back home, though the fiction that he would was played out for our sake. For days we hardly saw our mother. She slept at the hospital, in Dad's room, coming home only occasionally, and in a rush, to change her clothes and to see her children. Then, one morning, I woke to find her fast asleep in the spare bed, next to the double bed that Alan and I shared. She had come home in the middle of the night and had chosen to sleep in the spare bed, next to her children, not in our parents' marital bed. As soon as I saw her, I knew immediately that he was dead.

CHAPTER 5

A Woman in Charge

From 1942 onwards our mother was very much the boss, in charge of an ailing husband and her children, and working full time in factories. There was, of course, nothing unusual in finding women in charge in wartime Britain. Women at work, in factory and fields, became one of the visual clichés of British (and American) life during World War II. Pictures of smiling women, their sleeves rolled up and hair tucked safely away in turbans, working on lathes and tractors, were regular images in the press, propaganda posters and newsreels. With millions of men swept up into the military, great swathes of industry and agriculture – and indeed the armed forces – depended on female labour, much of it conscripted. As the war effort gathered momentum, it did so substantially through the efforts of the armies of women enrolled in war work. World War II – like the Great War before it – saw an extraordinary elevation of women in all corners of the economy, and to positions from which they had previously been excluded. Though the process was significantly reversed after the war, in the long term the female genie was effectively out of the bottle.

Though women were forced to step aside after 1945, to allow returning menfolk back into the workplace, the old arguments about the natural limits of female abilities and strength had been fatally undermined. The irony, however, was that women had traditionally been at the forefront of the British industrial economy. The cotton industry, for example – the origins of the Industrial Revolution – had from its inception been driven forward by female (and child) labour. In addition, there was one area where the dominance of women had never been challenged. They had always been pre-eminent in the domestic management of family life. All levels of British society left the domestic economy and child rearing in female hands. In working-class homes and communities, women in charge, dominant, even domineering women, had even been a basic and traditional source of jokes, music hall songs, fictional accounts and verbal banter. The tiny henpecked husband hectored by a large round wife, the harassed man seeking refuge from female domestic dominance among his mates in the pub, all this and more was the stuff of popular and graphic culture, from the saucy postcards of Donald McGill to the more recent Andy Capp comic strip. Caricature had been a mainstay of British cultural life since the mid-eighteenth century, its abiding popularity rooted in the fact that people recognised the simple realities behind the cartoons. Here were images which spoke to a particular reality, in this case, that at home women ruled the roost, though the limit to such dominance was obvious enough, notably the male breadwinner's control over family income.

As a small boy, on our regular trips to Blackpool, I loved to peep at saucy seaside postcards behind my mother's back. What made them funny was that I could actually put names to their anonymous characters: men and women whose personal lives were reflected in the postcards I loved. They reminded me of people I knew in the family and neighbourhood. One of my uncles spoke only when told to by his wife. For the rest, he sat there stoic and mute. Our Grandma imposed on her tiny house a pervasive grubby squalor which no one dared challenge. Some people even had appropriate nicknames to reflect their domestic arrangements. 'Whispering Grass' was a female neighbour who nattered endlessly, apparently without needing to stop for breath, her husband lifeless and speechless throughout. The man known as 'Bill Bailey' was so named because, whenever he dropped everything and departed to heed his wife's shrill summons to return home, people immediately burst into the song 'Won't you come home Bill Bailey?'. Closer to home, we had a dominant woman known behind her back as 'King Kong with Knickers'.

There was then nothing odd about dominant women, or about having women in charge, but what made our own situation different was our father's position. He had lost all the roles traditionally assigned to local menfolk. He was neither breadwinner nor manly figure about the house or neighbourhood. Our mother had, from 1942, to take on the role of both mother and father in the face of her husband's growing incapacity. She was, at one and the same time, the main breadwinner in years of general hardship, wife to a fading husband, mother to small boys, and constant nurse in the teeth of mounting medical crises. We grew up, then, in a household dominated by a fatally sick father and a powerful mother who was often stretched to the limits.

All this made for an unusual family chemistry, but at the time it seemed normal. It was all I knew. Although in my mid-teens I developed an abrasive, bolshie view of the world, and came to feel that we had been hard done by, the more I learned about the wider world in those same years, I eventually came to accept that we had got off lightly. How many other women, during that war and its immediate aftermath, were wrestling with similar circumstances – and much, much worse? Our difficulties were very personal, and not at all related to the devastation of wartime. Ours was just very bad individual luck.

Millions of women of that post-war generation – like their mothers in an earlier war – were confronted by difficulties which, today in the West, seem distant beyond recall. Though our mother did not have to deal with the emotional complexities of a returning soldier, her difficulties were immense and intractable. Her priority was a sick husband, and in a world of shortages and rationing, the best of the meagre pickings were reserved for him. My brother and I – fizzing with little boy mischief – did not always agree with this policy. The two of us occasionally sabotaged food reserved for Dad, and which Mum had acquired only after a lengthy queue. We once spread furniture polish on his favourite vanilla slice, and later lavishly soused his strawberries with vinegar. The sound of spluttering from his sick bed was followed by a prompt and richly deserved spanking for the two of us.

Being smacked was normal. It was not frequent or excessive, but common enough to be remembered. Our worst misbehaviour provoked something even more memorable: whacks, on the back of the legs, from a leather strap (a remnant of a machine belt, brought from a cotton mill by a relative specifically for the purpose). The strap hung on a nail behind the pantry door – a visible and daily reminder of the penalty for very bad behaviour. It wasn't used very often, but it dangled there, mother's nuclear deterrent, more powerful in its threat than its use.

Eventually Alan and I had had enough of it, and we buried it in the air-raid shelter, only confessing to our mother in middle age at a family wedding.

Today, these incidents seem strange. Our mother was neither harsh nor cruel but, like millions of her generation and earlier, she saw nothing wrong in smacking a child – actually she saw something quite *positive* in it. Of course most of her punishments stemmed not from any thought-out child-rearing theory but from hair-tearing exasperation. Coping with little boys in difficult circumstances clearly tested her to the limits – and beyond. I don't think we were especially mischievous, but even routine cheek and disobedience was more than enough for a hard-pressed woman. My own specialism was to be a verbal smart alec, replying to her annoyance with 'clever' (i.e. foolish) comments. I knew my remarks infuriated her more than Alan's more blatant mischief. And both prompted a clip or a smack. Even today, I can't say I blame her.

★ ★ ★

Our mother was the breadwinner, and the need to work, and to find extra part-time jobs to supplement poor wages, dominated everything. Daily life had to be fitted around her working day timetable. She worked at a range of jobs, normally more than one at a time. At first she worked in the hat factory in its steamy 'wet side', later on a conveyor belt in an electronics factory. Then there were more casual jobs after hours: sewing blocks of sergeants' stripes onto cardboard strips, working as a cleaner in shops, and later, long after Dad had died, hairdressing. She taught herself basic women's hairdressing, became good at it and by 1959 it was more lucrative than any other work she did. But it came at a price – for me at least. In my last two years at home, the house attracted a growing stream of local women, padding into the kitchen, which now served as a part-time hair-dressing salon: the same kitchen, same sink, which had been the location for such terrible scenes from our father's dying days. Mum was good at what she did, and she charged prices that attracted an expanding clientele of local women. In the process our home became a crowded, noisy crossroads, permeated by the sickly smells of hairdressers' concoctions, and dominated by the clatter of endless gossip – just when I had begun to study seriously, and when I needed a corner in a room, somewhere to be alone with books. I sought refuge across the road in Joe's spare front room and, even further afield, in the riches of Manchester Central Library.

In addition to these various earnings, from 1953 Mum received a weekly widow's pension. But until hairdressing came along, even when all this was added together it was rarely enough to cover the holes in the budget. My clearest memory of mid-week was of money having run out, along with most of the household food. The wages had gone, the pension spent, and there was nothing to do but wait for the next pay packet, or hope for a gift or a loan from a relative or friend. Sometimes we had to dip into my own tiny Post Office savings from my newspaper round. 'Hand to mouth' was not so much a common phrase as a graphic portrayal of weekly life. What clearly exasperated our mother most, however, was not the simple shortages – the predictable mid-week shortfall – but the pervading sense that there was no way out of the cycle. The fine balancing act of paying our way was regularly thrown by the slightest of incidents. The most basic needs – new clothes or shoes, or repairing old ones – simply tripped us up, though grandparents frequently bailed us out. Sometimes she had to postpone paying the rent (the landlord was our next door neighbour and was very tolerant about our debts). The most bizarre problem came via a small pay rise which triggered a loss of free school meals, though the problem was solved by a clever headmasterly ruse. All this and more – the regular pitfalls of the hand-to-mouth existence of poor people – regularly came along to complicate life. Nothing was more predictable than the uncertainty that dogged the weekly budget. Yet, time and again, we were hauled back by the intervention and help of others, notably by grandparents, and by the landlord agreeing, yet again, to defer the rent to a later date.

My brother and I noticed this in the most obvious and tangible of ways. When the money ran out, we went onto meagre rations. But the person who bore the full brunt of all this was, of course, our mother. She denied herself so that we could have what was available. But her main burden must have been the constant anxiety of not knowing from week to week how she was going to manage. Not surprisingly, she seemed permanently busy. She rarely relaxed and seemed not to have any obvious hobbies or time off from the tasks that dominated her life. She didn't attend church, or indeed any other institution or social gathering outside the house. Her life was one big bustle, as she moved from one task to another – caring for Dad, looking after her children, going to work. Hers was a life of unrelenting drudgery, with very few breaks or obvious moments of pleasure. True, people around us all worked long and largely unrewarding hours. But Mum's seemed an especially onerous existence.

She seemed to get pleasure from her children – when, that is, we were not testing her patience by mischief. But it was plain enough that whatever pleasures and happiness she and our father derived from each other's company had drained away in the wretchedness of his condition. They could no longer go anywhere together – even the local cinema was a struggle for him. And at some point even the happiness of physical love and intimacy must have ceased.

I only fully began to appreciate the unhappiness of our mother's life many years later. The more I thought about it, the clearer it became that there was one person with whom she found some comfort and solace in the midst of all this toil. She turned, of course, to Uncle Joe.

* * *

As children we had every reason to look woebegone and obviously poor. But we didn't. Despite everything, our mother took great pains to ensure that we were well turned-out. Family photos invariably show the children smartly dressed. Even at an early age I was captured wearing a tie. Yet the more I've scrutinised those photographs, the more perplexed I've become. Most of them were taken on high days and holidays, at the seaside, at church events and processions, or at family celebrations when we were caught by relatives who owned a camera. Others were taken in photographic studios. But whatever the occasion we were dressed in our best. Smart jackets and shorts, good sensible shoes, clean shirts and ties. Those pictures of our childhood are real enough, but they are totally misleading in many respects. I can't recall a single photo of myself and my brother capturing what we were *really* like. Most show us dressed for the occasion, dressed, in fact, for the camera: dressed how Mum would like us to be seen and how she would like our childhood to be remembered. Family photographs show few signs of everyday life. It was as if the camera deliberately disguised our real lives behind an image of well-dressed respectability.

We normally posed for the camera wearing what everyone called their 'Sunday best'. Our own 'Sunday best' was acquired each year, in time for the Whitsuntide church processions. Sometimes our clothes were bought by grandparents; at other times they were actually rented for the occasion from a local outfitter. Looking smart, putting on a good appearance, was particularly important at Whitsuntide when parents dressed up their children in new clothes, parading them before relatives and neighbours, then lining us up in church processions.

Whit Sunday itself came in two parts. First there was the curious Manchester ritual of visiting neighbours and relatives to show off our new clothes, and in return we were given gifts of small change. The pennies and small coins gradually accumulated as we did our morning rounds, and by the end of the day it amounted to a tidy sum which we squirreled away. Later that same day we took part in the church and Sunday School parades, with lines of children – all in new clothes – snaking behind church banners and bands. There is one cringe-making photo of me, in 1956, carrying a banner proclaiming 'God's Garden' – a reference not to a divine interest in gardening known only to a church in Failsworth, but to the ranks of little girls walking behind me. All this was a Manchester tradition dating back to 1901, of parading Sunday school pupils under the banner of their church. But always in their Sunday best. Alan and I, like most of the others, paraded in our smartest clothes: jackets and shorts or sometimes suits, school caps and ties. In some of the pictures, we could be mistaken for boys about to board a train for their first term at prep school. The photos are, then, both misleading and revealing. Though we looked nothing like that in normal, everyday life, our Whitsuntide appearance provides a telling insight into some of our mother's most cherished values.

Our generally smart appearance before cameras, was just one aspect of a deep-seated cultural regime which our mother (and legions of working women like her) insisted on, and which shaped the way we lived. It mattered *very much* how we looked when we were out and about. It also mattered how the house looked, both inside and out. Appearances counted. How we behaved in public, and at the table, how we spoke to our elders, how the house appeared to people casually walking past. All this wasn't a question of trying to look 'posh', but it was important that people (many of them sharp-eyed observers of the etiquette of local life) should detect nothing less than respectability in the way we presented ourselves, even though, as Grandpa Wood often remarked, 'You don't have a penny to scratch your arse with'. Notwithstanding that weekly high-wire act of making ends meet, though perhaps our precarious finances even accentuated it, the emphasis on appearing respectable in the eyes of others coloured everything. It affected how we were dressed and the way our hair was combed before we left the house. Before we stepped outdoors, our mother even inspected the inside of our ears – hurriedly cleaning them with the corner of a hankie if they were not up to standard.

There was never a moment of the day when appearances didn't matter, and our mother was permanently vigilant to ensure that nothing let her down: not the house, not her children – not even her milk bottles. Indeed this urge to respectability seemed to focus on the empty milk bottles on the front step. Putting out an unwashed milk bottle was a give-away sign: undeniable evidence of a slovenly householder, and a hint of the dirt lurking inside. Needless to say, our doorstep was never shamed by the presence of a dirty milk bottle.

Mum's concern about appearances began at the doorstep. Scrubbing, cleaning and 'donkey stoning' the front step was an essential feature of any clean house, and a way of letting others know that the house itself was clean. Yet, I often asked her, what was the point of her endlessly scrubbing the front step with a 'donkey stone' when, within minutes, it would be trodden filthy again? The unspoken issue of course, was not merely the finished product – a clean front step – but the fact that the woman of the house should be *seen* cleaning it. Such public displays of domestic virtue established a woman's local reputation. A mere glance at an ultra-clean front step, with its array of gleaming milk bottles, revealed the woman of the house to be a master craftswoman in the arts of keeping up appearances. By contrast, a mere glance at others in the street, only yards away, revealed a jumble of filthy bottles cluttering their front door. Theirs was an example of domestic fecklessness reflected in their milk bottles.

In all this, our mother was the polar opposite of her own mother, and perhaps this explains our mother's obsession. To Grandma Wood the act of cleaning seems to have been an alien exercise which she shunned at all costs. She simply didn't care what people thought about her house or her own appearance, and she shuffled through life with an air of harassed neglect. Her daughter, on the other hand, regularly worked herself into a froth to ensure that the house was clean, even when it did not matter (though in truth, it *always* mattered). Even when the most detailed inspection could reveal no blemish, Mum would storm through the house cleaning. She not only needed a clean house, but it was important *to be seen* cleaning it, and suitably dressed for the task. Here was a woman who, however many other distractions and chores she faced, became the patron saint of domestic cleanliness. The end result was that Alan and I shuttled between contrasting universes. We spent a great deal of time at our grandparents, mainly at weekends, in the process stepping from mother's spick and span cleanliness to the ingrained squalor of our grandmother's midden (her daughter's description).

Keeping up appearances in the public eye was only one aspect of mother's complex rituals of behaviour. She was a stickler for 'good manners', and they were to be observed at all times and wherever you were. At home, manners focused on the dining table (in fact a small table tucked against the wall in the all-purpose kitchen). We were frequently reminded how to eat properly, not to sit with elbows on the table, not to talk while eating (in fact not to talk *at all* when dining). Mealtimes resembled a trial to become a Trappist monk. The golden rule – this a universal wartime and post-war rule – was to eat up. It was a mortal sin to leave food untouched on your plate. The meals placed before us were basic and spartan in our early years – and especially when Dad was given the best bits. There was a calendar of dishes at mealtimes – a rhythm to what we ate. When Dad was alive, you knew each day what the meal would be. My particular horror was Tuesdays when tripe was served. The sight of it, soaked with vinegar, or cooked in milk, quivering on my parents' plates disgusted me and, to this day, thoughts of it prompt a feeling of nausea (even when it's offered in tempting style in French restaurants). Throughout, and for all the obvious reasons, culinary simplicity reigned. Various permutations of Spam (cold, fried, grilled, and frittered) and corned beef (cold or cooked as a hash). We ate food that was easily and quickly cooked after a long working day. But if one dish reigned unchallenged it was the potato. It dominated the table, most spectacularly at weekends at Grandma Wood's Sunday lunch. Her meals consisted of a mound of potatoes, streaming with Bisto gravy and, hidden away, a few straggles of chewy meat. My French pen friend could hardly believe his eyes. 'Les Anglais mangent seulement les pommes de terre!' he sighed, as he refused Grandma's offer of a lavish second helping of mashed potatoes. Vegetables, both at home and at Grandma's, appeared in lifeless form, all colour boiled and drained away: 'If I knew you'd be here this early, I'd have put them peas on an hour since'.

Special occasions demanded more lavish meals of course. 'Teas' took the form of a heap of sandwiches made from various meat and fish 'spreads', salads that were merely lettuce and tomatoes with a dollop of 'salad cream', and, on especially bountiful days, tinned salmon: a treat which quickly established itself as a much anticipated delicacy. 'Afters' tended to be tinned fruit (always topped with evaporated milk) which became increasingly common as rationing eased. In fact throughout my childhood I had no idea that peaches and pineapples came in anything other than tins. All this was accompanied, throughout, by endless cups of tea – with biscuits to round off an indulgent afternoon.

This was the age before the tea bag, and tea leaves were saved, left to dry on the draining board, then used and reused until all taste and colour had been leached from them. They were then scattered on the floor and used to dampen down the dust at sweeping-up time – ideal for keeping dust to a minimum in the face of Mum's manic dervish-like assault on household grime.

Throughout all these meals – at home, in Blackpool B&Bs, and at family feasts – my brother and I were expected to remain silent, not allowed to speak unless spoken to. Most curious of all, for reasons I never discovered, Mum insisted that when we ate at formal meals in other people's houses, we *stood*, even though there might be a profusion of chairs. Equally mystifying at the time – but much more annoying – she also insisted that we automatically refuse offers of second helpings, however abundant the food, and however hungry or greedy we felt. Both of us longed to devour some more peaches – or indeed anything else on offer – but it was thought rude to accept a second helping when first offered. The hostess would generally persist, wear us down (not too difficult), and ensure that we did indeed accept a second helping. In our mother's eyes, good manners demanded a polite, first refusal. I could make no sense of it at all. It was a ritual which seemed odd and, in any case, flew in the face of my natural greed.

Today, I find it easier to explain. It was yet another element in our mother's highly tuned, but very personal, sense of protocol. She did not want people to think her children greedy, or eager to gobble up food when others, less well-mannered and hesitant, might eagerly step forward. It may of course have originated in wartime and post-war scarcity, but it continued well into the 1950s when shortages had finally disappeared. Once she had put down a marker of what was, and what was not, acceptable it became an unspoken rule. Like the shiny milk bottles, the clean front step and the smart clothes – it was all of a piece: part of a pattern of private and public behaviour which defined who we were and how we lived.

Yet there was a glaring contradiction in all this. Everyone knew the reality: that we lived in the company of the legendary church mouse, but Mum was not about to have people think that we were anything less than respectable. I think the two were linked. The poorer she felt, the stronger her determination not to look down-at-heel, but to appear, on the contrary, respectable. If you wanted to find justification for what our mother insisted on, you need only look a few yards down the street to see the behaviour of feckless neighbours: grubby undisciplined children in dirty clothes, unwashed milk bottles clattering at the doorstep, and, at church parties and communal spreads (the Coronation being the most spectacular) children who guzzled away, elbowing aside more timid children, and wolfing everything in sight, until halted by a vigilant adult. You'd never find Cissie Walvin's boys behaving like that – or so she hoped.

CHAPTER 6

The Baby

In the autumn of 1960, in the company of other student friends, I avidly followed the *Lady Chatterley's Lover* obscenity trial at the Old Bailey. The trial, between the Crown and Penguin Books, is now famous as a landmark in publishing history, and a victory for literary freedom and for removing antiquated restraints on artistic expression. The six-day trial was a strange mix of high intellectual and legal debate, and bar-room vulgarity and farce. The case was peppered with bizarre and (from today's viewpoint) scarcely believable flashes of outdated social and cultural attitudes. Mr Justice Byrne summed up, agreeing with the Crown's leading counsel, Mervyn Griffiths-Jones that the jury should not allow themselves to 'get lost in the higher realms of literature, education, sociology and ethics'.

The courtroom discussions about the use of foul language (was the book obscene and therefore not to be published in its full unexpurgated edition?) and the ponderous, moralistic and heavy-handed conduct of the Crown's case, was a source of endless undergraduate discussion – and hilarity. Most of my friends were baffled by the courtroom debates about the use of obscene words in the original version of the book: words that were no different than those you could hear on student coaches to and from sports events, or late on Saturday night in the student bar.

As soon as the verdict went in Penguin's favour, and the unexpurgated edition could be published, with the offending words restored to the original version, our university bookstore opened cartons of copies, ordered for just that moment. In anticipation of winning, Penguin Books had stockpiled 200,000 copies around the country. Over the next two years they sold 3.3 million copies. I bought a copy for 3/6 (17½p) and read D. H. Lawrence's *Lady Chatterley's Lover* for the first time. I couldn't for the life of me see what the fuss had been about.

The novel, about a war-damaged man, unable to provide his wife with physical love and bowing to her passion for another man, had been subject to detailed forensic analysis in court by a host of expert witnesses. As I followed the trial in the press, and through all our late night student conversations about the trial and about the book, I was uncomfortably and secretly aware of the real-life echoes of the novel in my own family story. The irony, in our case, was that the man who had been damaged by war – Joe – was the lover, and the husband – my father – had stayed at home, unscathed by warfare. They were, of course, utterly different stories, but the similarities were still obvious.

At one level, the issues in the book and at the trial were universal human dilemmas. But they were also problems created by twentieth-century warfare, and it struck me that the experience at the heart of the book – the emotional torments of post-war lives – must have been much more common than people recognised. There must have been legions of people able to point to the emotional and moral turmoil in their own family life which reflected the issues in the novel. I suspected too that the people involved, like my own family, were deeply reluctant to talk about them. In the autumn of 1960, however, even to suggest that there was a parallel between the Lady Chatterley saga and my home life would have been to invite ridicule. For the time being, it remained an unspoken family secret. I was not yet ready to talk about it, even to my closest friends.

★ ★ ★

Our mother had become pregnant in the year before our father died. The new baby – my brother Ian – was promptly captured in family photographs. What makes the first photographs of the new baby special is that these are also the last pictures we have of our father. They show a gaunt man, aged beyond his years, lovingly cradling his third son. Family photos from a few years later, however, reveal a very different story. Ian as a little boy was invariably photographed with Joe Eyre: sitting on Joe's Rudge motor bike, in Joe's back yard or outside his house, mostly with Joe's arm around him. In fact most of the pictures of Ian as a child are taken in Joe's company. The photos also reveal that Ian looked remarkably like Joe.

Fast-forward the story another half century, and the images are even more startling. Ian as a late middle-aged man looks exactly like Joe at the same age. Not just similar, or passably alike, but *exactly* like him. Happily married, surrounded by five daughters and an ever-expanding brood of grandchildren, Ian is a replica of Joe at the same age. Today, we all recognise the glaringly obvious: that Joe was Ian's father. Coming to terms with that simple fact was a difficult and painful process, and was not fully resolved until our mother had died. Before then, it had been one of those unspoken family secrets that is really neither a secret nor unspoken.

Older relatives clearly knew, but said nothing. We were very young, and no one said anything in our presence: there were few hints or furtive gossip that might have prompted our curiosity. Years later, I gleaned a few snippets, all confirming what I began to suspect in my mid-teens: that everyone knew about Joe and our mother. Everyone had an opinion about it, ranging from the most flared of outraged nostrils through to sympathetic understanding.

In her later years, our mother became unusually moralistic and censorious, tut-tutting about various moral shortcomings in the world at large. When I mentioned this to my very old grandmother, her reply was blunt: 'I don't know how she dare. Not the way she carried on with Joe Eyre'. So there we had it: out of the mouths of babes and very old ladies.

For 50 years the question of Ian's parentage was a painful, troubling issue, likely to cause family disruption, stress and personal unhappiness, so my generation tiptoed around the topic, fearful that open discussion might cause hurt. It was discussed furtively between spouses, between brothers, and within my own family. It was a classic skeleton in the family cupboard, familiar, in different forms, to any number of families, and which finally emerges into the light of day with the passage of time, when the people involved have died, and when passions have faded. Sensitivities also changed. What once seemed shocking – unmentionable even – now seems inconsequential. Today, we all know and accept what happened. But for years after 1952 it was a raw, emotional issue.

★ ★ ★

It is not too difficult to see how Joe and our mother found comfort with each other. As their lives became increasingly entangled, they found the consolation they both needed. Throughout the late 1940s and early 1950s both were struggling with serious personal problems, and each needed sympathy and support. At one level, their problems seemed mundane. Mum faced the practical difficulties as head of a poor family in years of post-war hardship, while Joe had the humdrum problem of caring for an aged, disabled mother. But their difficulties went much deeper than this. Joe had to contend with his Japanese demons and the gruesome death of his wife; our mother was wrestling with her husband's decline in the midst of a young family. It clearly made for a volatile emotional concoction.

The liaison must have been difficult for all concerned, evolving as it did in cramped domestic circumstances. Each small house was home to a resident invalid. Our home, cluttered with noisy boys, centred on a sick man, unable to walk any distance, and bedridden for long periods. Joe's house, across the street, was also his mother's home: she was blind and disabled and unable to leave the front door. It was as if those two disabled people acted as sentinels at each house, feeble gatekeepers to a remarkable personal saga. Such awkward practicalities were, however, merely the most obvious of problems facing the lovers.

Joe was committed to his mother in a way which outsiders found puzzling, but which ultimately were rooted in the war itself. Once he had settled back home after 1945, once his wife had been cremated and he was able to get back to something like normal life, Joe made a commitment to his mother. He promised her that, whatever happened, he would care for her to the exclusion of all others. She was now his main concern. For years she had prayed for his safe delivery from Japan. In return, Joe promised not to leave the woman who had stuck by him when everyone else had given up hope. True to his word, nothing henceforth would deflect him from his resolve to care for his aging mother. Not even the love of another woman. Then, in 1952, a new baby appeared.

★ ★ ★

For much of the year before Ian's birth, our father was utterly incapacitated and confined to bed. At his weakest, he was fed liquids though the spout of a special feeding cup. Not so much at death's door but peering through it as it slowly opened. All this was hard for me to miss. I was getting older and more alert, and finally realised that he was dying, even though his chronic sickness had been at the centre of family life as long as we could remember. As he lay in bed, week after week, his condition clearly deteriorating, an air of misery descended on the house, despite the pretence, played out for the children's sake, that he would get better. His loved ones and his sisters turned up more often, and I noticed that the women, my aunts and grandmother, often left his bedside distressed, drying their eyes. The menfolk tended, of course, to be more stoic and unbending – but quiet. They all knew what was coming, and it wasn't too hard for us to realise what it was. But then, in the midst of this terrible decline, a new baby appeared. Today I think of it as an extraordinary life-affirming blessing – a healthy new baby arrived just when an older life was fading away.

For all that, it is hard to believe that the pregnancy was welcome. Life was hard enough without another mouth to feed. Months of pregnancy, then a baby, could only add to our mother's burdens, and all in the shadow of Dad's steep decline.

At a time when Dad could only be fed when someone raised and cradled his head, is it likely that he could have managed any physical intimacy with his wife? For long periods he seemed barely alive. Yet this was the year of Mum's pregnancy. What was said between the two of them when she discovered she was pregnant? What went through Dad's mind, as he held the new baby, realising that he would only know the child for a very short while? And what was said between the two men involved? Two boyhood friends, drawn even closer together by a baby born to one of them, but fathered by the other. All this remained hidden from our view and these undercurrents never broke surface. I was never aware of any reaction to the new baby other than delight at the arrival of a healthy child. Though it was another mouth to feed, most importantly, we all loved him.

* * *

In the early summer of 1953, the protracted regime of caring for a dying man was promptly replaced by the familiar routines of baby and child care. Our mother, no longer with a sick husband, now had to cope with three sons. I was now of an age where I could help, and in the years immediately after our father's death, many of the routines of childcare often fell to me. Mum could not afford to be absent from work or be late, and now in my teens I regularly took time off school for domestic chores. It was my daily job to wake Ian, get him ready for the day, take him to nursery, and later to primary school, before heading for the Manchester-bound buses and school. When he was sick, I simply skipped school to look after him. My school knew about our domestic situation and was always understanding, none more so than the headteacher, Sam Hughes, who was to prove a heroic figure throughout my secondary education. Through all these domestic distractions, I never felt that I was missing out by being absent from school. There was simply no alternative. The family breadwinner had to work, and it was my job (as Grandpa Wood would bluntly point out at Dad's funeral) to help make that possible whenever Ian had the usual infant and childhood illnesses. In any case, it allowed me free time at home with my books. Along with Manchester Central Library, those housebound sessions, alone with my books and a sniffly little brother, gave me the freedom I enjoyed to read and to work on my own. I now feel that I may have been better off reading and teaching myself than being in class.

For seven years or so after Dad's death, through all of Ian's early years and mother's (initially unsuccessful) financial balancing act, Uncle Joe remained a regular presence in and around the house. Eventually I got to know him better than I had known my own father. But in many respects he remained a mystery. Though the reality was slow to dawn on me, all the evidence suggests that Joe was in love with our mother, and that they had settled into a regular everyday relationship. Yet there was something unusual – something coy – about their liaison.

Joe paid court to our mother in his quiet, unobtrusive way. Though he showed great affection for Ian, in many ways Joe seemed to have bottled up his emotions, though in that he was a man of his times. All the men I knew – my uncles, my grandfather, close friends and neighbours – were people who did not openly display their private feelings. (Hence my astonishment at the sight of old soldiers weeping at the Armistice Day service.) To be stoic was a manly virtue. For that generation, and their sons, being a man involved knowing how to rein in your feelings. Joe was typical, but in his case the habit was forged and tempered by Japanese imprisonment and by his post-war bereavement. He was a man of great restraint which no amount of provocation could ruffle. The nearest he came to open anger was inevitably on matters Japanese.

Japan, the Japanese, the war, the post-war Labour government's supine failure to secure adequate compensation for the POWs – all these issues sent him into an icy silence. He visibly tensed, and said even less than in his normally terse conversation. It was clear enough that, for all his outer calmness, a mix of visceral hatred and anger stewed just below the surface. But it rarely became vocal or loud. He simply contained it. Throughout my teenage years I can recall only one flash of anger from him, and that directed at me, when I'd foolishly stayed out after midnight with some local mates, and Joe was dispatched by my mother to track me down and order me home.

Despite this emotional coolness, his feelings towards Ian and towards Mum were unmistakable enough. The flowers gave him away. Though Joe no longer had the excuse of seeing his old friend upstairs, he was a regular visitor to the house. Now he came to see our mother, and at weekends he often brought her a small bunch of freesias, her favourite flowers. Would a man of his age regularly turn up at a woman's front door clutching a bunch of flowers, in full view of curious neighbours in our dour working-class community, without some hint of emotional involvement? Yet Joe, a bunch of freesias in his hand, was such a common sight that I did not question it. I realised he'd visited by the smell of freesias in the house. Even today, the smell of freesias reminds me of Joe Eyre.

The real curiosity, the enigma at the heart of this story, is why a prolonged courtship that rumbled on for years did not turn into marriage. As far as I can tell, all the basic ingredients were there. Both Joe and our mother were clear of any attachments: Joe was a widower, Mum was a widow. They had a steady relationship – of sorts – and had a child. For an undemonstrative man, Joe displayed all the signs of being in love with our mother. He took a close, affectionate – paternal – interest in Ian. All the pictures of Ian and Joe together are effectively those of a father and son. A total stranger looking at those pictures today would simply *assume* they were father and son. Why, then, did Joe and our mother not marry?

Many years later, when I had finally mustered the courage to ask my aged mother, she told me that Joe simply never asked, so that was that. But why didn't he? They had every reason to marry, and to make formal what was casual though steady, and was obvious to everyone around them. My guess is that Joe intended to marry her eventually, and I'm sure Mum would have accepted, if only to escape her life of drudgery. But it never happened. For years I have scratched around for answers, and time and again I'm drawn back to the war, and to the personal turmoil of 1945–46.

★ ★ ★

In common with millions of others, Joe's late wife had found herself adrift, her husband apparently dead, vanished into the maws of an all-consuming war. She did not even have the consolation of knowing what had happened to him. 'Missing presumed killed' must have been the most devastating of messages, leaving a sliver of uncertainty hanging over surviving loved ones. 'Killed in action' meant that life for others could continue, in its grieving fashion, but 'missing presumed killed' created a life of suspended animation for the survivors. While Joe's mother lived in faint hope, turning to her faith for comfort and reassurance, his wife took another route. Joe was dead, and she needed to get on with her life. But then he turned up, as if back from the dead. Who could blame her – then or now – for the path she took?

Joe, his wife and her unknown unnamed lover lived out this personal tragedy in one corner of northern England. But they were merely one tiny example of what was happening worldwide, as millions of people struggled to piece together lives shattered by warfare and upheaval. Joe, understandably devastated by his wife's departure, never really recovered, and his deep wartime and post-war wounds – not the bullet wounds in his leg, nor his damaged eyesight – affected him to his dying days. He emerged from the wreckage, resolved to care for the one woman who *had* stuck by him through the bleakest of times, and whose daily prayers had somehow worked. As long as his frail mother lived, Joe could not commit himself to another woman.

And so it was that Joe and Mum got along – lovers, parents to a growing child, an 'item' in modern parlance – but denying themselves the comforts and pleasures of a permanent partnership and marriage.

★ ★ ★

Soon after our father's funeral, his older brother Jack and his family emigrated to Australia, returning only once, in 1976, for a last look at their birthplace and their surviving relatives. They also went to see Ian, then in his twenties, for the first time since he was a baby. When Ian opened the door, Jack's wife Lena blurted out 'Joe Eyre!' – the likeness was so stunning, so striking. I tentatively asked Jack about the whole saga of Joe, Mum and the baby. Without a hint of disapproval, Jack simply said that our father knew, and didn't mind.

He knew but didn't mind. Was he content to see his wife find the comfort and happiness which he could no longer provide, with his oldest friend? Jack's explanation seemed to confirm what I had felt, privately, in the autumn of 1960: that the three of them had, without knowing it, lived out their own complex but highly personal version of the Lady Chatterley saga. But I kept my thoughts to myself.

CHAPTER 7

My Grandparents' World

On the morning of the funeral, 11 May 1953, our father was brought home from the Oldham hospital where he had died, and placed in the front room. The undertaker invited friends and relatives to take their last view of him before he sealed the coffin. My brother and I were excluded, Mum feeling, wisely, that we ought to remember what he had looked like alive – though in recent months that wasn't saying much. Just as we were all ready to move off, Grandpa Wood took me aside and walked me into the back yard for a word of advice, man to man – my 11 years to his 63.

He wagged his podgy finger at me. 'Tha must remember. Tha's got to look after tha ma now. So don't forget – chin up!' And with that, he turned on his heel, and walked back into the house to join the funeral cortege heading to Rochdale Crematorium. And that was that: the sum total of grievance counselling for the young in Failsworth in 1953. Though Grandpa Wood was always a man of few words, his advice – even by his taciturn standards – seemed a little stark.

Over the years I've told that story many times to different people. Some were surprised, others quite shocked by what seems such blunt advice delivered during the most delicate and painful experiences any child could have. American friends in particular seem shocked by it. Yet I never thought of it in that light, at the time or since. Despite the bald simplicity of Grandpa's language, I now think of it as good advice, from a man of few words who always got straight to the point. I knew exactly what he meant. I was now the oldest male in the house and henceforth would be expected to shoulder some of the domestic burdens. I didn't question what he said, nor did I think it odd or wrong, even though today I wouldn't dream of saying the same to a child in similar circumstances.

* * *

The protocols of local funerals and mourning were very different in 1953. Alan and I sat in the front car with our mother, joined by Dad's brother, Uncle Jack Walvin, though some relatives thought his presence there upset the etiquette of the proceedings. Of all the emotions of that day, what sticks in my memory most vividly, was the *public* response to our passing cortege. Neighbours and local shopkeepers all stood silently at their front door as we drove past. For the first few hundred yards, there was not a single doorstep without a silent householder paying their respects by merely standing there. Even miles away, at the sight of the cortege total strangers simply stopped what they were doing, and stood, silent and immobile, until we had passed. In an age of almost universal hat-wearing, men instinctively removed their hats – cloth caps or trilbies. Here were people abiding by traditions which today – with the exception of royal and state funerals – have utterly disappeared.

After the funeral, we adjourned to a café in Failsworth, with the assembled friends and relatives tucking into the funeral tea of boiled ham (a treat then) accompanied by tiny silver-skin pickles, known locally as 'burying pickles' as they always appeared at funerals. Grandpa Wood, whose fingers on one hand were useless after being crushed in a factory accident, wolfed his food – as he did every meal – with his one good hand. He was seated at the epicentre of grief, between his widowed daughter and his wife. Both women were understandably disconsolate and weepy. Neither was hungry. Grief, however, did not diminish Grandpa's appetite. First he ate his own, then his wife's, and finally his newly widowed daughter's meagre plate of food. Replete, he leaned back and pronounced, in his wonderful Oldham accent, to the assembled mourners: 'Well! I've really enjoyed myself'.

Wails and sobs erupted from the women at his side, followed by weeping and eye-dabbing on a theatrical scale.

'How could you say that?'

'How could you say you enjoyed yourself when we've just buried our son-in-law?'

'You're a silly bugger!'

It was water off our Grandpa's back, and though he tried unsuccessfully, in his usual gruff fashion, to retreat from his mistake, it was to be thrown back at him for years to come, though normally in jest: a reminder and illustration of his tact and social delicacy. As I grew older, I came to admire his bluntness and his direct way of dealing with the world.

Grandpa was a tiny man. I've tried to calculate his height from the evidence of his photo sitting behind me, now, in my study. Standing outside his front door in Oldham, back to the wall, he only reaches the level of the 20th brick: I reckon that to be well below five feet high. He regularly trotted out the same old joke about himself: 'You don't find diamonds as big as bricks'.

What he didn't mention was that his height had been his salvation. Like millions of others, he had rushed to join up in 1914, but his height let him down, and he was rejected on medical grounds. He went back to the cotton mill, and by the time conscription rolled round in 1916, his work in cotton was deemed essential war work. Saved by his height, a characteristic he passed onto his grandsons, this tiny man was to emerge after 1945 as a marvellous but often unrecognised champion to his daughter and to us, his grandchildren.

Grandpa Wood was a late Victorian, born into a world where working–class children and adolescents shouldered burdens that, today, would shock the Western world. He had left school at 13, acquired a horse and cart, and set himself up as a general cartage and removal man. One of his first jobs at the age of 13 was to transport a family's worldly goods from Oldham to Blackpool. His working life, however, had been dominated by cotton, and by work in the *Elk* cotton mill. Every day he rose very early to walk the few miles to work, then, on arrival, he took a 30-minute nap on a bale of cotton before the machines began to turn, and the factory filled with the infernal racket of cotton production, the atmosphere fluffed with snow–like cotton. This airborne cotton (like the coal dust in the mines) was the cause of serious respiratory disease and it eventually saw Grandpa off, along with untold thousands of his fellow workers. He spent each sweltering day walking up and down the oil-soaked floor, watching cotton compact around a roller, then lifting and removing it when full. When I was 16, he showed me and my French pen-friend round his workplace; two 16- year-old boys, both sure of their physical strength, tried to lift the cotton roller – and we both failed.

This working regime shaped the whole of his life. He always rose early, at weekends and even when on holiday, and walked. In my childhood I spent a lot of time in his company – which meant heading off, at dawn, for a walk. Holidays made no difference and he always dragged me along. We let ourselves out of the seaside boarding house before anyone else stirred, and set off wherever the mood took him. Grandpa, a muscular man, marched ahead, while I struggled to keep up. At Blackpool and Southport we strode up and down the promenade, in Llandudno we skirted round the Little Orme – all before breakfast. Wherever we went on holiday, I normally shared Grandpa's bed, as I did when we spent weekends with them in Oldham. (What the usual sleeping arrangements were between our two grandparents I have no idea.) He never *asked* if I wanted to join him on his early morning walks – he simply assumed I would. Thus every day of my childhood holidays invariably began at first light, dragged from bed by my energetic grandfather, the next few hours spent scurrying to keep up with him. He was clearly at his best in the early light: one of nature's breezy folks to whom early morning cheeriness came naturally, greeting other early risers, or those returning from night shifts, policemen and busmen, as we burned off a couple of hours, and built up an appetite for breakfast.

Without our grandparents, and their son, Uncle Jack Wood, there would have been no holidays. We always formed part of that communal trek to the Lancashire coast in the company of many thousands of other Oldham cotton workers at 'Wakes Week'. Such popular seaside holidays were largely invented in Lancashire and had, by 1900, become a fundamental tradition throughout the Lancashire cotton towns. Factories closed down, local shops followed suit, and churches and chapels were forced to unite, bringing together the few scattered remnants of parishioners who stayed behind. Oldham had been at the forefront of this annual communal surge to the coast – and that meant primarily Blackpool. That once tiny fishing village had, by 1900, become the first working-class seaside resort. All this reflected the spending power of cotton workers: my own grandparents, like thousands of others, put money aside each week into a holiday savings club for their annual seaside trip (much as they put aside pennies each month to pay for a decent funeral).

With a few exceptions, we went to a favourite Blackpool boarding house, which was filled, like most of the others up and down the same street, with friends and workmates from home. Oldham, like other textile towns, effectively closed down for two weeks (the original one week growing to two weeks after the war), the entire population migrating along familiar routes, to very familiar resorts. It was as if we all hunted in packs: travelling, holidaying and enjoying ourselves in the company of people we knew, from the same streets, parish and factories. The journey itself was part of the holiday; packed into motor coaches ('charas') or crowded excursion trains – all filled with tobacco smoke – and all of them a travelling cacophony of communal fun and raucous excitement.

Behind us we left deserted streets and empty houses, the cotton mills silent and stripped, repaired and reconditioned by engineers, to be made ready for the workers' communal return two weeks later. By my mid-teens, when I opted to stay at home to work or to study, it was like living in a ghost town. I used to cycle round the town looking – mainly in vain – for signs of life. It must have offered ideal pickings for burglars – though there wasn't usually much inside the houses worth pinching.

The way we spent our holidays created a deep sense of personal and communal security. Though we were enjoying somewhere different, it was in the reassuring company of familiar faces. Once at the seaside, we were spoiled for choice for amusement. In addition to the crowded beaches and the sea (icy on the warmest of summer days), light entertainment was plentiful. All the major popular stars of radio, and later TV, appeared two or three times each day at Blackpool's massive seaside theatres and piers. We even saw them close-up, and waved to them as they ostentatiously drove up and down the prom between shows in big open cars. Today it seems slightly tacky, but at the time it was wonderful.

Our grandparents also took us on trips to London, first, to the Festival of Britain in 1951, on overnight trains from Manchester – again in a large local group. But our main trips to London were for the annual, men-only weekend escape, organised by the local Liberal Club, to the Rugby League Final at Wembley. My Grandpa took me first in 1956, and we stayed in Piccadilly, at the old Regent Palace Hotel, but even here, his regime was unbending. Up at dawn, across Piccadilly, down the Mall to the Palace, through the parks, and then back, through the still deserted streets of the West End, to the hotel, invariably arriving before the first waitresses were on hand for breakfast. He and I would wait impatiently for the restaurant doors to be opened, the first to the breakfast table, and the first to place an order. And invariably with Grandpa's trademark cloth cap plonked in the middle of the dining table. In the West End, on early Saturday and Sunday morning, his cap was as good as a neon sign announcing the presence of a working man from the north. I tried, politely, to encourage him to smarten up his act: 'Grandpa! *Please* – take your hat off the table!'. But to no avail.

Holidays came, then, courtesy of our grandparents. But so too did a host of other things: items which, as children, we simply took for granted. New clothes at Whitsuntide, weekend pocket money, even the food for Christmas lunch. Yet our grandparents had little money of their own and, in many respects lived in starker conditions than ours. Their house was certainly more basic. The outside lavatory was an old-fashioned 'tippler' which collected human waste until accumulated water from the kitchen rushed from the house, and tipped it over into the sewers. The house itself was in a shabby condition, poky and damp, and though the physical fabric of the place was grim enough, the real problem was Grandma Wood herself. This fat, roly-poly little lady, the most loving of grandmothers, ran the filthiest house I've ever stayed in. Though the smelly gloom of her domestic grime was off-putting, staying there was always offset by her smothering affection for her grandchildren, and brightened by her regular throw-away malapropisms. She could be relied on to lighten the darkest of Oldham days with her verbal contortions:

'I'm not paying the rent this week. Them kitchen walls are running with condescension.'

'I can't stand that advert showing dog food filled with Marylebone jelly.'

Hers was a house that might have been the origin of the old joke: so dirty that even the mice wore overalls. Gran couldn't cook, she didn't clean, her chamber pots would have disgraced a medieval army, and she never seemed to shake off that oily smell of the cotton mill. Yet she loved us and spoiled us – and we adored her in return.

Our mother railed against bad language, threatening her sons with fire and brimstone if anything rude tripped from our childish lips, but her own parents had no such qualms. One particular swearword cropped up regularly in our grandparents' vocabulary. Both of them used the word 'bugger' a great deal. Grandpa used it for every part of a sentence; its variants could be a verb, a noun, an adverb, an adjective – you name it, Grandpa would find a way of adapting it.

'Bugger off.'

'I'm buggered.'

'You know bugger all.'

'I buggering well will do it!

'Well – bugger me!'

'That's a bit of a bugger.'

'I'm really buggered [tired].'

A non-native speaker would never have guessed that the word 'bugger' was a swear word.

Grandma in particular offered a perfect illustration of how a swear word loses its power and meaning by regular, repeated or inappropriate use. She denounced all wrongdoers thus: 'He's a rotten bugger'. But she applied it indiscriminately to all and sundry:

'Grandma! The milkman's forgotten you today.' 'He's a rotten bugger.'

And – most spectacularly – 'Gran, did you know, that Hitler killed millions of Jews?' 'He was a rotten bugger.' It was hard to dispute that – but the milkman?

Our grandparents' social life was very limited, and was defined by the house, the neighbourhood and occasional shopping expeditions to Oldham or Manchester. I loved shopping with Grandma in Oldham's Tommyfields Market on cold winter days when she rewarded us with a glass of hot Vimto. Grandpa Wood's only reading material was the *Daily Herald* and a newspaper about horse racing. His bets were collected by the illegal 'bookie's runner' who slipped furtively in and out of local houses. I never saw Grandma read a single word of any kind. She could barely spell. Her inscription inside a copy of *The Cruel Sea* which she gave me for Christmas in 1952 reads 'Happy Ecxmas'. They were both regulars at the local cinema, the *Gem*, and of course we went to variety shows as part of our seaside holidays. Grandpa enjoyed football and rugby matches and the occasional pint at the Liberal Club. But that was about the limit of their leisure activities. No church, no books or magazines, no social groups. Theirs was a very restricted life, defined by work, annual trips to the seaside and weekend sporting events. Their home life improved a little in the mid-1950s with the arrival of a gramophone bought by their son, Uncle Jack, whose collection of 78s filled the house with Al Jolson's crooning.

As children we spent long weekends, holidays and regular day visits in their company – especially when Dad was very sick. But then, in my teens, when I developed a growing curiosity about history, it struck me that my grandparents – and indeed everyone around them – did not have much to show for all their hard work. What *really* puzzled me was that they, and more or less everyone I knew, were all convinced that we, the British (though they really meant the English) were the lords of all we surveyed. They assumed that we were the most exceptional of people, whose superiority was manifest in a variety of ways: in the way we ruled great swathes of the globe, and had, in their lifetime, seen off our enemies in two world wars. Throughout the post-war years of my late childhood and adolescence I cannot recall a single person, relative or friend, who did not subscribe to a general view of British pre-eminence and superiority. It popped up in all sorts of ways, and at the most unexpected of moments. Someone would mutter a casual banality about foreigners, about 'abroad', or about the latest crisis in foreign affairs, and others would nod agreement, or add their imperial pennyworth.

As I became seriously interested in history, the flaws in this outlook looked ever more obvious, and curiously seemed to find their focus on my grandparents. What had this great empire done for them, or for my relatives and our neighbours? My grandparents lived simple, often impoverished, lives with little to show for a hard week's work except a couple of shillings deposited in the holidays savings club, and the few pennies set aside in the local burial club. Their meagre pleasures seemed a poor reward for their part in an imperial success story. What did we all have to feel superior about?

I clearly remember raising these objections at my grandparents' home – aged about 16 – only for them to be roundly dismissed. My ideas were rejected as evidence of the dangers of education, and of reading too much. Grandma in particular seemed especially concerned about my reading habits. She even warned me directly: 'You mustn't read too much, our Jim. You'll get a brain tumour.' Her evidence for this amazing belief was the sad tale of a local boy who, having passed his 11+, promptly died of a brain tumour.

Despite his doubts about many of my judgements, Grandpa was quietly pleased with my progress at school, with my prizes and reports, though as always his pleasure tended to be registered low on the Richter scale of happiness. A couple of gruff words of congratulations, a silver coin as a reward, then back to mundane reality. But when it became clear that my school work might lead to something more serious, he marched me, unannounced, to Schofields, the best leather goods shop in Oldham, to buy a new briefcase. I was both astonished and delighted by the gift. I have no idea how much he had to work to pay for it, but it was a costly item which I treasured for many years. It served me in all corners of the globe till it finally gave up on me and fell apart in the Caribbean.

Both grandparents had their flaws, some of which only became apparent as I grew older. Grandpa had a volcanic temper, a risky habit in so small a man who was prepared to call the bluff of much bigger men. For her part, Grandma had been a flighty younger woman whose love life, I was to discover, was more colourful than it should have been, and clearly caused Grandpa deep unhappiness at times. But all of this belonged to an adult world which didn't impinge on our dealings with the two of them.

I now know that Grandpa kept back some money from his earnings to deal with family emergencies – of which there were plenty. His other daughter generated crises left and right: unpaid debts, court appearances for this and that, scrapes of one sort or another – all, and often at the last minute, ultimately sorted out by Grandpa Wood. All this, coping with the transgressions of relatives, his subsidising of our stretched family finances, was done quietly, with no conditions attached: no need for thanks or public acknowledgement.

I once innocently trespassed on his generosity. In 1956 I sent him a postcard from France, mentioning in passing that I thought France expensive. By return post I received a five pound note – which had not been my intention at all. But it was too late, then, to explain that my comment had simply been a casual throw-away line of no importance. I thanked him on my return, of course, receiving in return that snort and a nod which passed for acknowledgement, before he went back to his newspaper.

Throughout the 1940s and 1950s these two people provided us with a vital safety net, though even with their material help, life was basic. Without it, I suppose clothes would have had to last longer, holidays would have been fewer, and the food would have been even more frugal. I find it easy enough to outline the practical help our grandparents provided, but it is much more difficult to convey the moral support they offered. Theirs was as much an emotional as a practical safety net. In their poor, grubby and untutored home we found affection and emotional security which was as invaluable as the material help they provided.

* * *

That grey northern industrial world – the world I lived in, but especially the world I knew via my grandparents home in Oldham – quite suddenly became a focus of national interest. When I was in my mid-teens, that world became the object of widespread cultural discussion. It was at its most obvious in a string of novels, plays and films, and one major sociological study, Richard Hoggart's *The Uses of Literacy* – all offering different portraits of working-class life in the industrial north. The small gang of us who constituted the fifth form were urged by an imaginative schoolmaster to give serious thought to these various portrayals of contemporary cultural life which began to appear around us. Inexplicably, the only world we knew was now the centre of remarkable cultural interest and attention. It also coincided with my discovery – prompted by the same schoolmaster – of George Orwell, a writer who rang all sorts of bells for me.

This popular focus on working-class life in the late 1950s was a contemporary sensation, and it pulled me in various directions. On the one hand, I found much of the debate familiar and even obvious, and my teenage prickliness sometimes made me bridle. I didn't need John Osborne, John Braine or Alan Sillitoe telling me what life was like. On the other hand, I was quietly pleased that the grubby face of life as we lived it was being exposed in all its sweaty reality. What genuinely confused me, however, was *why* working class life had become so popular and attractive? What was special and what was new about lives which were there for all to see? Why – now – was there such widespread cultural interest in the grey corners of English life which millions of people knew at first hand? It felt as if alien anthropologists had descended on English working-class life to explain what many of us knew by instinct and upbringing. I didn't realise it at the time, but that is exactly what happened. Paralleling the novels, plays and films of those years, a string of sociological studies focused on working-class life in a variety of locations, from Leeds to Oxford, Bethnal Green to Hull.

The enthusiasm for 'kitchen sink drama' among (largely metropolitan) critics was, in reality, not new at all. The 1950s passion for scrutinizing the bleaker features of English life (and it was England rather than Britain) was merely the latest variant of a well-worn pattern with very deep roots: the discovery and exploration of the 'other England'. Throughout the nineteenth and early twentieth centuries, a variety of critics had periodically revealed the harsh realities of urban and industrial life, and just as frequently, more prosperous society had recoiled in fascinated surprise at what was exposed. Indeed, local social history could be written via the investigations of generations of investigators, from the great social reformers of the early nineteenth century onwards. The list of those involved embraced some of the great writers and critics of the past century and a half: Dickens, of course, time and again, Charles Booth in London, Seebohm Rowntree in York. It was as if each successive generation needed to be reminded of the harsh realities of life around them.

What flowered in the late 1950s was slightly different, however, this time taking the form of a string of overlapping novels, plays and films based on the novels, but all blending into a broad cultural criticism of the way we lived. Of course the world scrutinized by creative writers – England in the 1950s – was utterly different from earlier English societies. This was post-war, post-Beveridge Britain, transformed by the Welfare State, yet still afflicted by a host of age-old social problems and attitudes. For all my prickliness about what was happening around me, I enjoyed everything I saw and read from this cultural smorgasbord, from *Room at the Top* and *Look Back in Anger* to *This Sporting Life*. I felt completely at home when talking about it. It was as if I were on home territory.

The one writer who impressed me most of all, the man who spoke most directly and evocatively to the world I knew, was Richard Hoggart in his book *The Uses of Literacy* (1957). Here was a book with a seismic impact that set in train another cultural wave, this time of social scientists, alighting on various working-class communities across Britain and offering new analyses of the current state of local working-class life.

Reading Hoggart, hard on the heels of Orwell, was a revelation, not so much in revealing something that was totally new, but in the way he spoke about a life I recognised. The book's focus was West Yorkshire, not Lancashire, and drew its social and intellectual inspiration from Hoggart's birthplace in Leeds. But that was less than 30 miles away, just over the Pennines from where I grew up. Though he wrote about different regional and parochial cultures and accents, what he described was uncannily like the one I actually knew. Hoggart's account of hearth and home, of family, relatives and community was, at one generation and 30 miles removed, recognisably my own. His description of his former home in Leeds could have been mistaken for an account of my own grandparents' house in Oldham. His words were all the more compelling because they pushed to centre stage the two diminutive cotton workers, my grandparents Robert and Carrie Wood, who had been so central to my entire life up to that point.

★ ★ ★

In these widespread public and scholarly debates about working-class life, there was much discussion about the nature of 'community' and how it functioned. It was –and is – easy to romanticise all this, and to sketch a sepia-tinged view of the good old days. But no one, confronted say, by Grandma's chamber pots, by our freezing bedrooms or our late father's haemorrhages into the kitchen sink, could possibly fall for that historical illusion. At times, I found myself confused by these discussions, largely because I tended to measure what I read against the experience of how my own family had fared. At the time, I didn't think that 'community' had played much of a role in the way we lived. We had bumped along primarily because of our mother's energy and resolve, but also via the help of a small, close-knit group of people, led by our grandparents, but including an ad-hoc number of relatives, neighbours and friends. It now looks very different. These same people were the warp and weft of a community which looked after its own through thick and thin.

CHAPTER 8

Friends and Neighbours

The house is still there, modernised by the look of it – no doubt now with the benefits of central heating and internal plumbing. It was very different then. Next to the end in a late Victorian terrace and slightly bigger than the houses across the road, it had the real advantage of backing onto open fields. As children we simply stepped out to play on the open land behind the house. Our landlord was our next door neighbour, who kept an eye on the state of his properties, and the physical fabric of the house was also much better than many others near by. Even so, it was a cold house, our only heat coming from coal fires and a kitchen stove. If you really wanted to visit a shabby poor working-class home, our grandparents' house would have fitted the bill. From their house in Oldham, row upon row of small terraced homes radiated out like spokes on a wheel, creating an almost Lowry-like caricature of working-class northern homes. Though our home was cold and austere, there was nothing slum-like about it. It was nothing like the houses I passed en route to school, large Victorian piles in Moss Side, divided into flats, packed with Irish immigrants (who were being rapidly replaced by people from the West Indies). Ours was stark, but not obviously impoverished, in large part because of our mother's relentless efforts to 'keep on top of things', to use her own phrase. The house was simplicity itself: a two up two down terrace with steep stairs up the middle, turning left or right into a bedroom. Downstairs a front room looked out onto the street; at the back an all-purpose kitchen overlooked the back yard. The front room, the 'best' room – what some people called a parlour or sitting room – was supposed to be reserved for special occasions (the most special being Dad's coffin taking pride of place for a few hours under the front window). We lived mainly in the kitchen, which was the focal point for family life, not least because a corner stove kept it warm. It was also a meeting place for all the human traffic flowing in and out of the house. Close neighbours often came directly into the kitchen via the back yard, and our mother's women friends regularly gathered round the kitchen table, a tea pot plonked in the middle, in what looked, as they swivelled the tea pot from one to another, like an interminable game of tea-time roulette. The kitchen was always noisy, always a place of bustle and activity, and smells.

Everything seemed to take place in the kitchen. We washed there in the morning and ate there at mealtimes. Mum cooked there, of course, and stored food there as well as in the under-stairs pantry. The weekly washing was done in the kitchen, and the laundry dried dangling overhead from the kitchen rack. Once a week, on Sunday nights (even, as the old joke had it, when we didn't need to) we bathed in the kitchen, in the zinc bath which normally hung on a nail outside the back door. When we were small the boys were bathed together, but as we grew bigger we bathed separately, the one inheriting the grey and rapidly cooling water from the other. Finally – as if the kitchen did not have enough uses – in the late 1950s Mum was to turn it into a back-room hair dressing salon.

The bedrooms were plain, but above all they were *cold*. My pet dislike was the bare linoleum which drained away the body's heat when you swung your legs out of bed in the morning. Our parent's (later, our mother's) room had better furniture – the bedroom suite they had bought from the Co-Op at the start of married life. Our back room was simple, basic even. In my teens, and to escape the crowd in the kitchen below, I tried working in the bedroom, but there was only a small dressing table with its large mirror, and I found myself spending more time gazing at myself than my books. So I invariably slouched off across the road to work in Joe's front room.

It was from just such a bedroom, on the other side of the street, that Grandma Walvin had been involved in a macabre saga, years before. Along with another woman, she used to lay out the local dead for people who could not afford the full services of an undertaker. Once, when her work partner was sick, she called on her elder son, Jack, to help her carry a dead man downstairs to the kitchen for preparation. Jack took the naked man's legs, Grandma lifting the man under the arms. As they turned sharp left to go down the stairs, then doubled up the corpse to get him round the corner, the body gave out a loud deathly belch. Jack – first time on the job – dropped the bottom half of the body in terror and fled, leaving his mother stranded with a naked corpse halfway out of the bedroom.

Local custom reserved the front room for the best furniture. Or rather, in our case, what had once been the best furniture before it fell victim to the routine battering of small boys. We were supposed to keep out but didn't. Centre stage in the front room was occupied, in turns, by the radio, the Dansette record player and then, in 1960 – and finally catching up with millions of others – a television set. Later, the furniture also fell victim to Alan's ingenious money-raising schemes. He prised the furniture fabric free from its frame, to find the loose change which had fallen into the body of the chairs. This source of income, along with cash diverted from his school dinner money, provided funds for his first Woodbines.

The back yard was dominated by our father's isolation shed which became ideal storage space for the accumulation of household and children's clutter. A few feet beyond was the coal shed and, finally, at the far end of the yard (in the most distant and therefore most inconvenient spot) lurked the outside lavatory. It was, like all such, a miserable place. I had totally banished it from my mind until, many years later, I encountered my first Australian outdoor dunny, and the dismal memories came back. Our lavatory did not encourage you to linger, certainly not to read – not least because there was no light. One of the delights of my first year as a student was discovering the pleasure of indoor lavatories, especially at the homes of student friends. Warm, lighted, and equipped with a washbasin and even pictures, books and magazines, they were far removed from the cold, distant lav (which froze in bad winters) and which was stocked, not with books, but with old copies of the *Oldham Chronicle* in lieu of toilet paper. One of our favourite little boy japes had been to hurl a metal bucket down the yard when our mother was in the lavatory at night. Her squeals of alarm at the sudden crash in the outside darkness was our reward for the devilment. In such uninviting conditions, calls of nature were inevitably answered swiftly: a brisk trek down the yard for as brief a visit as possible. Older folks, less nimble and slower, had to resort to our grandparents' habit of placing chamber pots strategically round the bedrooms. Installing an indoor lavatory (alongside the all-conquering washing machine) was to transform life beyond measure.

An unkempt garden lay beyond the back yard, and finally, the small air-raid shelter. The garden yielded lots of rhubarb but for the rest it was a wilderness, untouched except when a distant uncle, a retired Derbyshire miner, visited and spent his holidays turning it over. When he left, it soon reverted to its native wilderness. Other neighbours took care of their plots, but ours went uncared for: Dad couldn't do it, and after he'd died, Mum had no time, and her children were too young or not interested.

The house itself was, of course, the main playground for three growing boys. Ian was a small child throughout most of this time and didn't generally figure in the life and games which Alan and I shared together. Only three years apart, we were naturally close throughout our childhood, until we both went our own ways in 1960. As young boys we played together, slept in the same smelly double bed and talked each other to sleep with stories and fantasy tales. We scrapped, of course, and at first (being older and bigger) I usually won, until Alan began to outgrow me and was able to get the better of me. Thereafter I decided there were less perilous ways of dealing with him.

Whatever our boyhood squabbles, we were united on one main issue: the need to defeat Germany. Although in the world outside, the war was rapidly receding, it remained a hot topic between the two of us. We shot down more German aircraft than all other RAF aces combined. Our fighter aircraft consisted of two kitchen chairs, laid on their back, with me (the pilot) slotted in the front, Alan (the navigator) at the back. The plane was amazingly manoeuvrable: we could pitch and roll simply by leaning left or right, Alan unfailingly guiding me onto the German target with sharp-eyed warnings picked up from the films we'd seen: 'Bandits at two o'clock!'.

We reigned supreme in the skies above Failsworth, with so many Huns crashing in flames that it was surprising that the town wasn't totally destroyed by falling German wreckage. When not beating the Germans in the air, we attacked them on the ground. For that, we practised parachute drops, jumping feet first from a raised corner of our bedroom onto our double bed. Like many real life drops, it came to a sticky end: Alan crashed through the mattress and bed, and neighbours had to be roused to extricate the squealing child from his predicament. Thus ended our threat to the Third Reich.

Not all our games at home were so boisterous. I was especially keen on making things from cardboard boxes, but sliced off a small tip of an index finger in the process. We enjoyed the usual childhood toys – lead soldiers and a Meccano set, which grew over the years into a massive collection until, aged 13, I sold the entire kit to a friend at school and spent the money on books. Our real playground, however, was outdoors. Throughout our entire childhood, I can recall no sense of concern or worry about allowing children to play outside, in the streets, or in the fields behind the house. We were free to play and to roam. For a start there was little danger from traffic. Our mother showed no real unease about our long absences from the house. We were *never* told that wandering the streets was at all risky, and that we should beware of this danger or that. We generally felt free to stay out as we pleased, though we normally told Mum where we planned to be. We used that freedom to play the traditional street games, team games, and learning traditional folk rhymes and chants. Years later, I was amazed to discover that the very words we chanted had been faithfully recorded and published by two eminent folklorists, Peter and Iona Opie.

> Down in the jungle
> Living in a tent
> Better than a prefab
> No rent!

> I say, what a smasher.
> Betty Grable's getting fatter.

That dated us precisely to the post-war building of prefabs and the popularity of Betty Grable, but we also chanted rhymes with a longer vintage and without knowing their historical significance.

> The moon shines bright on Charlie Chaplin
> And his boots are cracking
> For want of blacking
> So they're going to send him
> To the Dardanelles.

All this was innocent enough, but some of our games *were* risky. In very hot weather, the most dangerous fun was swimming in the Rochdale Canal, fast clogging as an industrial artery, and the general muck and rubbish around the canal deterred me from ever joining the tougher lads who dived in. More dangerous still was the game of 'Duckie'. We piled broken bricks into a mound, leaving one boy to guard them, while the rest of us scattered and hid. He had to spot us (each of us armed with a half brick) then touch the pile, before we could knock it down with a brick thrown from a distance. Hurling a brick at a target guarded by another boy inevitably led to accidents, though the wonder is that they were not more frequent or more serious. I once split open a boy's head with a misdirected brick, and had to sit, contrite, before the stitched-up victim, fresh from his medical treatment, as my mother plied him with apologies and cake.

These games, the folk customs and rhymes of children across the country were, like life around us, also the subject of serious investigation by Peter and Iona Opie. All the rhymes and chants, the team games and play we enjoyed without question, many of which were largely inherited from older generations, were carefully noted and recorded by the Opies. When I later discovered their work I was reminded of games and verses I'd long forgotten. Here was yet another sharp reminder of how much scholarly and cultural attention had been paid to the world we lived in as children. Our material and family life was discussed by sociologists, the emotional lives of adults laid bare by playwrights, and even our childhood hopscotch captured by folklorists. Though none of us were aware of it, it now seems that we were the objects of intense social curiosity from all angles.

★ ★ ★

The people around us were a varied bunch of working people, and ranged from quiet church-going folk through to the totally dysfunctional – brawling, and shouting both at home and in society at large. Two of our neighbours were brothers who fought all the time, and even had a spectacular scrap in a Sunday School class. Our mother's neat and tidy home became my early yardstick for judging others, and I was always surprised to discover neighbours who lived quite differently, but happily. Some were totally at ease in conditions of permanent chaos. One large family at the end of the street appeared never to clear up, their house dominated by a kitchen table permanently piled high with dirty plates, rib bones scattered between the plates as if vultures had recently passed through (which, after a fashion, they had). Yet they seemed a happy bunch, presided over by a large jolly father and his fat, equally jolly, wife. They could easily have been the urban equivalent of the Larkins in *The Darling Buds of May.*

At the other end of the street, however, at the other social extreme, another large family lived out a caricature of the Irish poor: a boozy dad, a permanently pregnant wife and an ever-increasing brood who squabbled about everything. We were totally bamboozled one Christmas morning when the children knocked on the door offering to sell their newly opened Christmas presents. The boys who were my age were tough and fearless: they were the first (and last) to dive into the Rochdale Canal on hot days. They scared me, and my determination to steer clear of them was made easier by the fact that they attended a distant Catholic school.

The very poorest local family lived across the street. Like us, they had a disabled father, and the house (what our mother primly called their 'midden') was overrun by neglected children. Yet in the midst of all this, the damaged jewel in that bleak home was their Down's syndrome son. He never learned to speak, issuing instead a stream of jabbering noises, but he was, throughout, a deeply affectionate child. He was a regular visitor to our house and became very close to our father, partly I think because they were both at home so much. The boy would simply burst through the front door unannounced, leap onto a chair and begin his lonely incomprehensible jabber with Dad, who would reply patiently in what he thought was the mood of the conversation. I used to find these scenes deeply upsetting. An affectionate child, trapped in his compound disabilities, desperately trying to communicate, and laughing with, a very sick man. The child was deeply upset when our father died.

Despite his problems, the boy also had a boldness about him. He got into endless scrapes because of his fascination for motor vehicles and travel. He liked to join a bus queue and simply clamber onto a crowded bus, all the passengers assuming he was accompanied by someone else. When they reached the terminus, the driver and conductor found themselves in charge of an empty bus and a very happy Down's syndrome child sitting at the back. The return journey was interspersed by the conductor leaning out and asking whether anyone knew this child. Finally he was deposited, delighted with the day's excursion, at his starting point. Newspaper delivery vans offered similar temptations. The van would stop for a minute, the driver hurriedly unloading a bundle of papers at the newsagent, giving the boy just enough time to dive through the open back door and hide behind a pile of newspapers. He was happily swept off on the delivery round, until discovered and returned.

The neighbours who really fascinated me most were the old ones. I was drawn to their company mainly because I enjoyed the stories about their early lives. Uncle Fred Ogden, three doors down, beguiled me with tales about his military service both in South Africa and what he called 'the Mespot'. An older female relative told of her pre-1914 part-time education: mornings at school, afternoons in the local cotton mill. Tales from an even older woman about her life as a 'Jacquard weaver' took me back even further to the local domestic textile industry. All these stories seemed merely absorbing accounts which caught my attention and which I stored away. What I did not appreciate at the time was that these various older people and other experiences (the soldiers at Armistice Day, Mr Clough's singing lessons) were providing me with small pieces of a historical jigsaw which eventually I would try to make sense of in a much more formal fashion.

★ ★ ★

There was one group of local people I never really got to know. The people we regarded as 'posh' were few in number, but were objects of great curiosity. We applied the term 'posh' very loosely, to people who seemed different – superior – in some way: people who had a little more money than most of us, who had a better sort of job, or whose outward signs of prosperity, such as a better house or smart clothing, marked them off from most other local people. There was, of course, a small sprinkling of local professional people, notably doctors, but they all lived in a more desirable area, and came to their surgeries by car. There was in addition the vicar's family, although theirs was not so much a 'posh' as a 'distressed gentlefolk' style of life.

The term 'posh' was also used as an insult, a means of dismissing people who were thought to have 'got above themselves', another of our mother's favourite phrases. One childless couple in the street, having been successful pub landlords, had sold the pub for a handsome profit, or so we believed. Thereafter they lived in a posh manner, though why anyone with money should choose to live in our street remains a mystery. They wore expensive clothes, and she radiated a snobbish disdain for the world at large. She certainly did not like me as I grew up. I thought her a haughty leftover from Edwardian prudery, and it amused rather than irritated me. For all that, years later she provided my brother Ian with an escape and a home when he needed to break away. Even more obviously prosperous was a local builder and his wife who lived in what we regarded as a grand house. They had a car and, rumour had it, even had a billiards table in the house. They were indisputably posh.

Apart from this tiny band of posh people inexplicably marooned among us, the very great majority of people around us were working people. Some were skilled tradesmen, and others held minor managerial roles (foremen, like Joe in the hat factory) but most were unskilled working people employed in the range of local factories – cotton, hats, rubber – or in the transport and service industries spawned by greater industrial Manchester. Together, they were part of a tight-knit working-class community which, like others of its kind, was defined and shaped by a number of major institutions: the workplaces, shops, places of worship, drink and entertainment, and schools. All were within easy walking distance of home. Our lives were, above all else, essentially local. Children went to local primary schools, families shopped in neighbourhood shops, and most people worked and worshipped locally. Even the weekend breaks from work were enjoyed close by: the cinema, pubs, the weekend pleasures of sport or family visits and (curious today) walks to and around the local cemetery. It had been decided to have Dad cremated some miles away in Rochdale to prevent our mother embarking on the popular ritual of a weekly trek to the local cemetery with flowers.

From working to worshipping, people lived out their lives in the company of folks they knew and who generally lived in the same cluster of neighbouring streets. We went to the local cinema as a family, normally joining a long queue of neighbours to get in. Women shopped, cared for each others' children, and invited each other round for tea. Pubs filled with men who knew each other, from round the corner or from work. We set off together on Saturday to watch the same sporting events, and we even made the annual trek to the coast together, on the same trains or coaches, and ended up together in neighbouring boarding houses. There was a parochial, an almost tribal, feel to the way we lived.

We even talked about ourselves and defined ourselves in very local terms. Though we lived in an extensive urban sprawl which stretched from northern Cheshire to the Pennines, people tended not to stray far from their own neighbourhood, largely because there was no need to. Everyday needs were catered for by small retailers and shops dotted around the local streets. Bigger stores in Oldham and Manchester were for special occasions and bigger items. We shopped at the Co-Op (I still remember our dividend number – 785), at the greengrocers and at a bread shop round the corner, all of them only yards from our home. The nearest newspaper shop was only yards away, across the street, and it was only a five-minute walk to the local fish and chip shop. Shopping and, in the case of children, 'running errands' normally involved only a short walk to buy a small number of things, or even a single item. The modern culture of buying large volumes of goods, in a single trip, was unheard of. As late as 1960, there were only 367 supermarkets in Britain, and I didn't use a modern supermarket until I was a student in Canada in 1964. We shopped, just as we lived and worked, locally, day by day, acquiring what we could afford (restrained until well into the 1950s by rationing) and what was needed for the next meal or the next few days. There was of course no domestic refrigeration in most households, and we kept perishables in a larder and in a cabinet with mesh doors.

Naturally enough, some people chose to break away from these communal routines, preferring their own company, or opting for different individual ways of living and enjoying themselves – they were often thought of as 'stand-offish' as a result. Apart from bikes, and except for those, like Joe, who had a motor bike, there was little private transport. We travelled everywhere on public transport, by bus, trolley-bus, trams (until they were scrapped), train and coach. Gangs of us boarded the same trains heading for the coast, and knots of neighbours waited to be collected by the coach, picking up its complement of holidaymakers and trippers from local rendezvous points. Most day-to-day travel, to work or to shop, was done on foot, for the simple reason that work and shops were local. All this began to change, however, in the mid and late 1950s.

Our first relative to have a car bought a precarious looking three wheeler in 1959, but I first noticed the increase in cars among teachers at school. About the same time, I enjoyed my first ever trip to Blackpool by car, in a small family car bought by my then girlfriend's father. That first trip by car marked a dramatic change, as we joined the traffic jam heading to the coast, chatting among the four of us. All my previous seaside trips had been with hordes of friends and neighbours, in a crowded coach or railway carriage: noisy, often boisterous, smoke-filled and invariably echoing at some point to communal singing. The car journey could not have been more different. It was as if travel had suddenly been privatised, and we'd left everyone else behind. These motoring memories belong to a much bigger picture. There were only 3.5 million cars in the country in the mid-1950s, but that had almost tripled a decade later.

Through all this, the main defining issue, obviously, was money. Women – housewives – bore the brunt of the regular routines of daily shopping, queuing, cooking and providing, but their most difficult task was juggling as best they could whatever cash they received from working husbands. Few people seemed to have enough cash to last more than a few days. There was a general taboo about openly discussing earnings and savings, but one curious aspect of our financial lives was open and largely unchallenged. Today it looks puzzling. Everyone I knew, and everyone I spoke to about the matter when I was in my teens, all told the same story. I knew no men who would admit to handing over a wage packet in its entirety to their wives. Men gave money to their wives for 'housekeeping'. I frequently met men who confessed that their wives had no idea how much they earned. It was a secret they simply would not divulge. Instead the breadwinner handed over what he thought was required to run the household. The major exceptions to this rule were young adults living at home, and working for the first time. It was assumed that they would give their wage packets to the woman of the house, who doled out a weekly allowance in return. When I first started vacation work in 1957, my wage packet was simply taken from me, and I received 'pocket money' in return. Though my summer earnings, from 1957 onwards, were meagre, even when augmented by overtime, they clearly made a huge difference to the family income. Eventually I began to feel that the few shillings in my pocket (from my pay for, say, a 50-hour week) wasn't a fair return, but I never felt able to challenge my mother about it. In most local homes, however, the main breadwinner – the man of the house – was exempt from this. He decided what his wife (and family) needed and what was appropriate to keep for himself.

★ ★ ★

In this tight-knit local world, 'helping out' was a way of life. Helping neighbours with mundane tasks, especially in times of crisis, was part and parcel of the way we lived. People helped each other as a matter of course, at times of sickness and old age. Though the new Welfare State had begun to improve life immeasurably, old habits of self-help and neighbourly care remained vital. These often took the form of the simplest of gestures. As children, Alan and I were regularly sent to older neighbours' houses simply to see how they were, and to ask if they needed anything. We were employed to 'run errands' for old people in the neighbourhood. It might merely be to fetch bread or a newspaper, but for the house-bound, infirm or old, it was a lifeline. The whole process was exemplified by our dealings with Mr and Mrs Ogden, old neighbours who lived three doors down. 'Uncle Fred' and 'Auntie Ogden' were a very old couple with no local relatives, who, in their last weeks, both declined rapidly together and relied largely on neighbours for everything. They both had poor eyesight and could not read easily, and I was regularly recruited to read the newspaper to them in the evenings. Other children shopped for them, and helped with other daily chores. Then, in the space of a few days, Uncle Fred suffered a stroke and was bedridden. His wife, already frail and infirm, could do nothing to help, so most of the necessary jobs fell to neighbours. But then she too had a stroke and died. Her body, awaiting the funeral, was laid out on a trestle table in the back kitchen. Fred, fading away and slipping in and out of consciousness, was cared for by a roster of friends and neighbours who sat with him, day and night, and this included me, then aged 14. My turn was the early evening shift. One day, I took the short cut and entered the house by the back kitchen door, forgetting the corpse was there. I was confronted by a large fat body, lying under a white sheet. But what *really* spooked me was the sight of a mouse, running along the full length of the body before disappearing into the pantry.

I sat with Fred for about three hours, talking a little when he was lucid – endlessly muttering 'I never thought she'd go before me' – before handing over to an older neighbour on the later shift. The undertaker delayed Mrs Ogden's funeral, knowing that Fred was dying, and expecting to be able to bury both man and wife in one ceremony. But Fred lingered, and she had to be buried alone. A couple of days later Fred died.

No one thought it inappropriate to recruit a 14 year old, if only for a few hours, to look after a very old man who was dying, with his wife's corpse lying a yard away. My mother encouraged it – I think she volunteered me – and no one objected. Like others on the roster, I had to help him in the most intimate of fashions (helping him, for instance, to urinate when he couldn't hold his penis in place). That, and worse, the routines of everyday care and nursing, was mainly done by friends and neighbours without objection or question. Though an extreme example, it was all real enough: an indication of that sense of obligation which local people showed to one another, which was at its most striking and selfless at the two extremes of life. Neighbours rallied to new mothers and similarly stepped in with the very old, no longer able to cope on their own.

All this was not so much a reflection of people's good nature, but stemmed, I think, from simple necessity. People helped, both knowing that it was the right thing to do, and that they too might have to call on neighbours when faced by occasional difficulties. Neighbourliness, for want of a better word, was a social requirement in a community of people with few resources. Though today I look back on that world with a degree of nostalgia, I also recognise that it was often an unrewarding world, where people needed and helped each other in ways that, today, have changed beyond recall. (I would never have allowed my own 14-year-old sons to care for a dying old man. Alone, with a corpse in the next room.)

There were, of course, plenty of examples of the less caring, harsher side to local life. Only days after our father's funeral, a neighbour knocked on the door asking for the dead man's clothes. Stunned relatives explained – truthfully – that all his clothes were destined for the incinerator as part of the need to purge the home of his consumption. But the request, and its timing – so cold and inconsiderate – caused anger which rippled through conversations for years. No one gave a thought to the miserable circumstances which drove the neighbour to beg for a dead man's clothing. It was simply seen as heartless, and his family was promptly dispatched to outer darkness – people with whom we had no further dealings.

Much more common, however, was unsolicited help and support from people around us. Although our mother was a robust and physically strong woman, both before and after our father's death the family could not have functioned without the support of other people. That assistance made her life easier, and made her children's lives fuller and more enjoyable. The key helpers were not always the most obvious, or the ones you might expect.

One abiding childhood memory is of a full house: three children with our own boisterous presence, our playmates, and an apparently endless parade of adults, mainly women, and Uncle Joe of course. Some of our 'uncles' and 'aunts', who were not blood relatives, merely close friends, were more helpful and more affectionate than some of our relatives, who might just as well have lived in New Zealand for all the help they offered. This pattern was true of many other local families, but in our case, with no father in the house, the role of our various uncles and aunts loomed much larger.

The inner circle was quite small. One uncle and aunt lived just round the corner; our grandparents and their son Jack were only a short bus ride away in Oldham. And Joe Eyre, of course, was only a few steps away across the street. This small group was regularly augmented by others who lived close by, and who proved important in the way the family bumped along. The people I remember most clearly are those who cared for the children. Though it didn't strike me at the time, most were people who had no children of their own. Alan and I (and later Ian, with other neighbours) became, in effect, surrogate children to childless people. Uncle Jack Wood, Mum's brother (there were Jacks scattered throughout the family) was a case in point. A single man who married much later in life, Jack clearly took a shine to me, whisking me off on holidays that were totally beyond our reach. First (by plane!) to the Isle of Man, then to the Channel Isles, where I rewarded his kindness by losing his Leica camera to a fast incoming tide. (I felt less bad about it when I discovered that he'd acquired it for a pound of butter in post-war Germany.) Like his father, Jack was a down-to-earth man whose broad Oldham accent turned heads anywhere outside the parish. This favourite uncle lavished treats and quiet affection – yet expected nothing in return.

Another (non-related) uncle was Ben Boardman, across the street. He had been a professional footballer with

Manchester City before the war, though we never held that against him. A regular dog walker who pounded the local streets and fields most days, and dragged Alan and myself along on long walks. Later we were taken up by Bill and Margaret Perry, also childless, who became our football guardians on trips to Old Trafford, and to more distant football matches. They welcomed us into their home and, like Jack Wood and Ben Boardman, were generous and caring in an understated undemonstrative way. In addition of course, but in a category of his own, was Uncle Joe, whose special concern was Ian.

Through all our various dealings with these and other adults, our mother had no qualms about allowing us to spend long periods in the care of other people. She clearly trusted them with her children. No doubt she was happy to see the back of us for a while, and to have some temporary relief from the rowdy presence of small boys. Perhaps too, in their turn, they felt sorry for our beleaguered mother. I suspect too that they would have loved to have children of their own, but life conspired against them.

I've often tried to explain to myself what these people got in return for looking after us for long periods. What possible benefits could they derive from the company of small boys? I don't think we were especially difficult children. Our mother's drill-sergeant regime ensured that we were, on the whole, well-behaved. She instructed us about good behaviour immediately before we left the house, and she quizzed us about our behaviour when we got home. Even so, we inevitably required the attention and effort demanded by all children. Perhaps we *were* surrogate sons, the children they could not have. Or perhaps they simply enjoyed the fun and amusement generated by the young. For us however, the benefits were clear enough: we were able to enjoy a much fuller life than domestic circumstances would otherwise have allowed. I can now see that, in the process, we became accustomed to the company of adults, and were at ease among people outside the family, developing a gregariousness and even a social ease with grown-ups. It wasn't planned that way, but the time spent with trusted adults proved a boon. No less important, our time away from home provided temporary relief for a young woman besieged by children and domestic worries.

Looking back from an age of controversy about child care, what stands out in all this is the *trust* involved. Our mother – and many others like her – trusted certain people with her children. Moreover, this trust went much deeper than child care. Trust was the lubricant of social arrangements in ways often overlooked by commentators. Trust between local people was the very means by which the whole community functioned. People needed to trust one another with all sorts of tasks. Even as small children we were entrusted with money, on errands for neighbours, especially for old people. Women trusted each other with a string of domestic chores, but above all, of course, they trusted others with the care of their babies, their children and, eventually, the care of the old. All this may seem commonplace, and in many respects it is. But trust was an invisible indefinable quality that lubricated the community networks of local working-class life.

Looking back on the wave of literature about working class-life which proliferated from 1957 onwards, there was much debate about the nature of working-class communities. In our specific case – one family beset by its own individual problems – the community that really mattered was small-scale and close-knit. At the time, I didn't think of the ties which bound us together as *community* ties: they were more bonds of family and friends. It was an irregular and changing group of people drawn together by need, affection and kindness. I came to feel that what had sustained the family I grew up in had been a small band of people who, in effect, formed a safety net which stopped us from falling further. Yet curiously we were, at the same time, part of a local set of networks which served as a support for others around us.

★ ★ ★

Apart from school, the one place which took up most of my time was St Johns, the local parish church, and its Sunday School. Until my faith finally drained away at 17, Sundays were dominated by the Church of England and by 1959 I had had more than a decade of being thoroughly drilled in the Anglican regime. Just as important, and by far the most enjoyable feature, I had sung regularly in the church choir. Why I was propelled towards the Anglican church as a child remains a mystery. Dad had been raised in the secular church and had attended its Sunday School very close to home, in a school hall opened in 1880, and Mum showed no signs of being particularly religious. Her parents did not belong to, or worship at, any church. Two things, however, led us to St Johns. The Sunday School was a very lively organisation offering a range of instruction and a great variety of social activities, and my singing attracted the attention of the church choirmistress.

The first hymn I sang as a choirboy, as we processed down the aisle in Failsworth in 1948, was 'Jerusalem, My Happy Home'. 'That's odd,' I thought, 'I live in Failsworth'. Until I became accustomed to the often tortuous phraseology of the Anglican hymn book, hymns created lots of similar confusions. It took me ages to work out why the green hill was without a city wall. And the

National Anthem ('Send her Victorias') left the obvious unanswered question: Why send plums to the Queen? Such confusions aside, singing in the choir twice each Sunday (Matins and Evensong) and on special occasions, and practising in mid-week, became regular fixtures of life. Sundays were simply set aside for church and Sunday School. I enjoyed singing and inevitably became steeped in the hymnology and liturgy of the Church of England.

Sunday School was the venue for a host of regular children's activities, and provided a crowded calendar of annual events: Whitsuntide walks, the annual Christmas pantomime, the summer day trip to the coast, and major children's parties on special occasions. Treading the boards in a St Johns' panto, and singing solo parts in the church choir, provided an early apprenticeship for a career which required me to sing for my supper in front of students and the public.

Sunday School also taught me to dance – after a fashion. As young teenagers we had dance classes – old-fashioned stuff, waltzes and tangos. It was to take longer for more energetic dances to raise the roof at St Johns. I was, and remain, utterly toe-tied, gormlessly uncoordinated and clumsy, and I envied friends who glided effortlessly round the floor. The only thing I *did* like about those teenage dance lessons, despite my faltering efforts, was the fleeting opportunity to hold a girl in my arms. One girl was especially busty, and holding her close, in the last waltz, was an early experience of sexual bliss.

Though it provided the rare opportunity of holding women, I went through life thoroughly disliking dancing. However, I once went with a gang of Sunday School mates to the New Years Eve dance at Manchester's Free Trade Hall. It was a curious mating ritual where young men and boys lined up along one wall, girls and women on the other, each side eyeing the other for prospective dance partners. In fact the very last thing I wanted to do was to dance and I simply could not muster up courage to ask one of those girls – giggling with her mates on the far wall – for a dance. My tactic was simple: I stood alone, my animal magnetism wooing them to cross the dance floor towards me – my allure made all the more irresistible, I hoped, by my matching knitted yellow tie and gloves. Oddly enough, they resolutely refused to head in my direction. And so, I headed back to Failsworth, undanced-with, on the early morning bus.

St Johns was, of course, another very local affair. Worshippers and Sunday School pupils were largely drawn from the immediate neighbourhood. Being the C of E, it also registered the peculiarities of the English class system, with some pews reserved for certain better-off parishioners. On Sundays a local tradesman shepherded his family into a front pew, his name discreetly registered on a small nameplate – 'The best seat in the house' according to a mate in the choir. They were *definitely* 'posh' because they lived in a semi, and the father went about his work in a van, rather than going to work, as did the plumber who regularly came to fix our outside lav, sporting a bag of tools over his handlebars. But even the rank and file non-posh dressed up for church, donning our 'Sunday best'.

Church services provided a splash of colour and ceremony in an otherwise grey environment. The regalia of worship and singing – gowns, surplices, starched ruffled collars and 'Sunday best' – all offered a stark contrast to the grey lacklustre attire of the working week. Special occasions such as Armistice Day, Christmas, Whitsuntide, Easter, and Harvest festivals when the church was decked out with foodstuffs, all contrasted with the dreary realities of life outside. But even here the evidence is misleading.

Surviving photographs of the choirboys, meekly lined up in V-formation at the church porch for weddings, give a misleading impression. We appear to be a group of well-behaved and tightly marshalled goody-goodies. In fact we contained the usual mix of boyish misbehaviour, teenage vulgarities and general monkey business. One lad claimed to have found an ideal place in church for a quiet wank before choir practice. I priggishly rebuked him with the obvious words 'Is nothing sacred?', to which he replied 'There's nothing more sacred than a good wank'. Since this conversation took place in church itself, and almost as if to prove that the Anglican liturgy had really imprinted itself on us, another choirboy ended the conversation with a loud 'Amen!'.

After church we quickly reverted from sweet-looking choristers to rough and tumble schoolboys. On the way home from choir practice, a fellow chorister loved to frighten women in the dark by creeping up close behind them before emitting the loudest belch I've ever heard. He once made an old lady visibly jump from about 20 yards. He was also addicted to knocking unexpectedly on doors and fleeing at an amazing speed, leaving the rest of us scattering for cover – but he was a Manchester City fan, so what could you expect? Needless to say, our choirboy talk, even in church, was the usual mix of schoolboy smut and gossip about life's great mystery (girls) and football. Yet from this unlikely and unpromising bunch, our martinet of a new choirmaster (who also played the organ at one of Manchester's big cinemas) extracted a decent weekly choral performance. By working himself into a phoney stew of anger and imposing some form of military discipline into our ranks, he managed to get us to sing well.

Much as I enjoyed churchgoing, and especially the choral singing, I had serious doubts about my faith from the first

– nagging, simplistic, but unanswered worries. As a small child I regularly prayed for Dad's health and recovery, but my prayers seemed to be answered only by a worsening of his condition. His death left me with a deep and unshakable doubt: one of those simple intellectual problems common to millions when confronted by personal disasters. All the obvious questions popped up. How could a loving God do this? That and similar questions recurred time and again throughout my childhood and teenage years. What had we done to deserve our hardships? What, for that matter, had Joe done to deserve his unhappy lot? How could you trust in a God who allows such terrible things to happen to decent people? In gloomier moments it made no sense whatsoever. All this was, of course, a naïve and simplistic questioning of the fundamentals of faith, but it simply wouldn't go away.

My faith finally vanished after discussions with our local vicar when I was 17, though I think that was the occasion rather than the cause of my loss of faith. Though the two rows of World War I ribbons pinned to his surplice earned my respect, I found him an aloof, nervous old man who was simply unable to cope with the persistent boisterousness of teenagers. I took particular umbrage at his support for capital punishment. I heard that he had officiated at executions in Manchester's Strangeways jail, and began to pester him about it. (Curiously, another man in the neighbourhood, Albert Pierrepoint, England's most famous hangman, ran a pub – appropriately named *Help the Poor Struggler* – only a mile or so from home. It was alleged that he installed a notice saying 'No hanging round the bar' until the Home Office ordered its removal.) What really troubled me was the vicar's firm conviction, expressed in ethical discussions in Sunday School, that capital punishment was morally *right*. Our conversations coincided with the mounting public debate about capital punishment. I found the BBC's habit of announcing those deaths on radio ghoulish: my grandparents, for example, tuned in simply to hear the announcement that someone had been executed. I simply could not come to terms with the idea of a man being executed in the presence of, indeed with the apparent *approval* of, the vicar of my church. The firmer the vicar's support for capital punishment, the more it eroded my faith which, already weakened, now simply drained away. I suspect now that after all the slaughter the vicar had seen on the Western Front, he found it hard to worry about the death of the occasional wrongdoer.

For all that, the Church of England left its fingerprints all over me. Its rituals, its calendar, its hymns and liturgy, all and more remain embedded deep in my brain. Today, there are times when I feel I am one of a dying breed of Anglican survivors. In recent years I have attended funerals where the only people in church who seemed to know the hymns, prayers and protocols were me, the minister and the organist. Those 10 years before the Anglican mast were, however, to be put to good use in a totally unpredictable way, many years later, when I immersed myself in the Caribbean. There, among utterly different people, but who were even more devout and more deeply steeped in Christian choral practice than I had been as a youth, my old Anglican sensibilities were revived. Though Jamaicans tend to be Nonconformist rather than Anglican, it was striking – odd at first – to feel at home among Jamaican country folk, in a village church, and to recognise the same habits, routines, and the simple ingrained religious culture of an earlier life, 5,000 miles away, in the industrial north of England. Yet even in the Caribbean the old confusions arose. Early on Christmas Day, 1968, in Lluidas Vale, Jamaica, with the temperature outside already rising above

80 degrees, the assembled congregation, myself included, struck up:

'In the bleak mid-winter, frosty winds did moan.'

It took me right back to 1948, and my confusion about Jerusalem and Failsworth.

CHAPTER 9

Learning

On the face of it, there was not much encouragement to read at home, where books were in short supply. We received Charles Buchan's *FA Book for Boys* as Christmas presents, and we owned a few dozen books, but they were all packed away in cardboard boxes in our bedroom, alongside the cartons containing the wartime gas masks. Our father had been a *Daily Herald* man, and the books had been acquired as part of a *Daily Herald* special offer: a one-volume encyclopaedia and a complete set of Dickens. Bound in false brown leather, and printed in unreadably small type face, the Dickens seemed designed to grace bookshelves rather than be read. Today they remain on my shelves – a sentimental reminder of my father, one of only three items of his in my possession, along with a pocket watch and a signet ring. I also had a collection of Dad's book prizes for regular attendance at the secular Sunday School he attended as a boy in the 1920s. They too were boxed away.

My own book collection began modestly enough, and, like Dad's, took the form of Sunday School prizes. The first was a Biggles book, and thereafter I bought new Biggles books whenever I had spare cash, and asked for them as presents. But my entire Biggles collection, along with Dad's books, went the way of a furious book clearance in 1960, shortly after I left home, in a foolish moment of frustration: part of the emotional confusion I felt in the wake of the family upheaval and turmoil that was happening at that time. It was as if I were casting aside childish things, and clearing the decks for more serious reading, but I suspect too that I needed to purge myself of the traces of a life that had been suddenly transformed.

All the books we owned were, then, hidden from sight: there was clearly no intention of reading them. There were, however, plenty of other books available, round the corner in Failsworth's Carnegie Library. My mother took me on my first visit and I immediately liked the place. I took to its distinctive smell of highly polished floors and desks, and best of all, the smell of books; to this day whenever I buy a book I sniff it. However, gaining access to Failsworth's public library alone, as a child, was not straightforward. For a start, the place had a forbidding appearance, partly because it shared the same red brick building as the local council offices, which to a child's eyes were quite intimidating. Most important of all was the question of cleanliness. To be admitted you had to extend the palms of your hands to the scrutiny of the librarian in change. If they passed muster, you were allowed in to handle the books.

The library was a turn-of-the-century building at the centre of the town, on Oldham Road, backing onto the Rochdale Canal, and overlooked by the Gladstone Mill. It took only two minutes to get there from our house, and it became the first of countless libraries I've worked in. Long before I went to secondary school, before I discovered Manchester and its great libraries, I developed the habit of slipping into Failsworth's library, finding a book, and retreating to a chair in the corner. Hiding away, surrounded by books, became a lifelong habit, but of all the libraries I've worked in, many of which impose all sorts of complex entry restrictions, Failsworth was the only one that demanded a clean pair of hands.

From the age of 11, I changed buses, coming home from school, outside Manchester Central Library and soon established a regular routine of working there in the evenings. At first I was in awe of the place, uncertain about whether a schoolboy should even be taking up the space. By trial and error, I learned that I could get more or less anything I wanted to read, either from the abundantly stacked shelves arranged in the outer rim of that huge circular building, or buried beneath us in the stacks, and all promptly available on application. I quickly developed a love for the routines of library work: waiting outside, early on Saturday morning, for the doors to open; finding a convenient seat after school in the evening (like most readers I developed that proprietorial attitude towards my favourite spot and regarded competing occupants as squatters); exploring the open shelves; applying for odd, obscure volumes. I learned too how to *use* books, not merely to read them, how to gather and assemble information. Here too I learned how to write – all taking shape under the great dome of the main reading room in Manchester Central Library.

My initial reserve about the place soon vanished in the presence of the very mixed and sometimes downright weird company around me. Here – and later in libraries all over the world – I found myself among all manner of eccentrics and misfits. It was soon apparent that libraries offer more than an endless supply of reading matter. They are the natural habitat of odd people the world over. The bewildered, homeless and aimless, smelly tramps and sexual perverts of various persuasions, or those merely sheltering from the rain or cold, all and more jostle for space alongside serious students. For a short while one regular in Manchester Central Library (smartly dressed and apparently a prosperous figure) was a farter on an epic scale, his unabashed Krakatoa-like eruptions caught on the acoustics of the domed ceiling and sent rippling round the library. Finally, the staff and his fellow library users had had enough and he was banished. Years later, in the wonderful New York Public Library on 42nd Street, a man facing me almost slid out of his chair, trying to lower his vision to look up women's skirts on the opposite desks. Another, in Manchester again, spent the entire day transcribing betting odds for horse races onto the inside of old Woodbine packets. Later, as a graduate student in Canada I knew someone who enjoyed exposing himself – but only in the theology section of the university library. Having to show a clean pair of hands to get into Failsworth library seemed a minor matter after all that.

* * *

Because of the war – and women's war work – my age group had been bundled off to primary school at the age of three, though each afternoon we went to sleep wrapped in red blankets on camp beds. I didn't shine at primary school but my singing voice was noticed early on and was often put to good effect. A small van delivered the school dinners (dominated by gristle and lumpy custard), and whenever it was delayed I was hoisted onto a school bench to serenade the school with a variety of patriotic songs and hymns. Instead of tucking into a grey-looking post-war school lunch, my fellow pupils had to listen to me trilling 'I Vow to Thee My Country'. The exercise killed both the time waiting for the food and my enthusiasm for patriotic songs. If they could be used to pacify hungry kids at Stansfield Road Primary school, what else might they be used for?

In a world of food shortages, we received a daily sermon from the headmistress about the importance of 'eating up'. One of my classmates, repelled by the particular food on his plate, refused to eat and was hauled onto the school platform, where the teachers ate while gazing down at the rows of children eating. The entire school was ordered to lay down knives and forks, and watch as the headmistress ordered the boy to eat. We all looked as he tried, but failed: instead, he vomited copiously across the teachers' dining table. At home, our mother preached similar sermons, but normally accompanied by a comment about China: 'Eat up! Don't you know they're starving in China?'. Smart alec replies about the Chinese being welcome to my Spam invariably invited a sharp clip.

The primary school lesson I hated most was knitting. We were all, boys and girls, busy knitting useful items – dishcloths and the like – but I simply could not get the hang of 'casting on' and 'casting of' and creating a fresh row. I thought I could get away with simply pulling and stretching the existing knitting, and presenting it to the teacher as if I had knitted a new row. She counted the rows, checked her list, realised I was lying, and whacked me across the head. Fortunately, the girl next to me was already a speedy knitter and helped me out; I thus stumbled through to the end of the dishcloth.

No one seemed to think it wrong to smack a child for a range of misdemeanours. We were regularly smacked, slapped, thumped and whacked – with fist, palm and by a range of hand-held objects. The fattest of our female teachers used to creep from the back of the class, between the rows of children. If she spotted any slacking, talking or doodling, she gave the offending child a fat-armed punch at the base of the spine. One of the male teachers – the former rear gunner we all thought barmy – used the blackboard T-square or a ruler to rap the knuckles of offending children. Behaviour that would today lead to dismissal and a court appearance went unremarked – it was an unexceptional daily occurrence. If you complained at home the reply was likely to be, 'It didn't do me any harm'.

For all that, it was a happy effective school which coped with a with range of abilities. We had a Down's syndrome boy in our class, a delightful child who proceeded at his own happy pace and who in adult life developed an extraordinary interest in and memory for pop music. He settled into a happy working life as a farm labourer. At school he was, inevitably perhaps, teased and taunted, 'Funny face' being the most common gibe. One day he had had enough, seized the main culprit, and slowly ground a piece of schoolyard coke into his face. It took a mighty struggle by four of us to overcome his titanic strength and extract his squealing victim.

The last year at primary school was dominated by the looming 11-plus examinations: that annual sorting of children into educational sheep and goats. The successful ones went off to the nearest grammar schools, the failures were dispatched to the roughhouse that was the secondary modern behind our house. The preparations, the mock exams and tests totally bamboozled me, and I worried endlessly about what would happen. When the examinations came, I was apprehensive and overanxious. My interest in libraries and books seemed to get me nowhere. I wanted to go to Chadderton Grammar School, but in the event failed the 11-plus. Though it is true that the preparations and the examinations coincided with our father's final illness and death, I can't really blame that for my failure. After all, I failed again when I resat the examinations a year later, when domestic life had reverted to a more settled regime. I doubt I would have done any better had I taken the tests at 18.

I was, of course, disappointed not to go to the grammar school and promptly became a signed-up member of the band of critics of that perverse and unjust system. As I grew older, and became successful at academic work, my initial disappointment curdled into a sense of social injustice and political anger. In the event, my failure at 11 proved a blessing. Instead of a grammar school or secondary modern I went to a 'technical school' in the heart of Manchester – a school with no academic pretensions but which offered me an ideal setting for my education. Located in Moss Side, then a poor immigrant area of the city, it was an unusual mix of a school, theoretically geared to educate boys of a more practical inclination: boys who might head towards apprenticeships or clerical work. More crucially for me, and a handful of others, it also had enough good teachers to encourage and guide us. And it had a sprinkling of bright boys who had slipped through the 11-plus net. Above all, we had a headmaster who had a knack for spotting pupils' various talents, and then pushing and encouraging them. His most spectacular success was spotting the acting potential of John Thaw. I didn't realise it at the time, but I also benefited from the simple accident of travel and geography. My bus rides home from school took me past one of the Manchester's great treasures, the Central Library, and it was there that my real education took place.

Predictably enough I went through life detesting the idea of the 11-plus and everything it stood for, curious about those who had breezed through it (especially those who simply peaked at 11), and scoffing at those colleagues, years later, who were major proponents of grammar schools and of testing children at 11. As it happened, my secondary school suited me well, and what shaped my teenage education were books, Manchester Central Library and a few devoted schoolmasters.

★ ★ ★

The school passed through a variety of names in my time there. Formerly known as Ducie Central School, it became by turns Ducie Technical High School and Ducie High School. It catered primarily for boys who were deemed to fall between grammar school and the secondary modern. In the arcane and divisive language of the time, itself rooted in the dubious science of IQ testing, Ducie's pupils were not heading towards 'academic' interests. We were thought best placed behind a lathe, a joiner's bench or a clerk's desk. Although I learned how to weld metal together, and to make a mortise and tenon joint, I was happier with a book. By the mid-1950s, however, it had become abundantly clear that the school's pupils had a wide range of talents and Ducie began to offer more 'academic' streams for small numbers of boys. Then, when enough boys secured good O-level results, the decision was made to develop a sixth form. By the time I was 16, a small trickle – only two or three each year – were managing to secure places at university, most of them in north-west England, in a range of disciplines. Among the boys I knew who went to university between 1957 and 1960 all secured sparkling undergraduate and graduate degrees – in medicine, psychology, physics and history. And all of them 11-plus failures.

It was equally clear that there were many more who could have benefited from higher education if the chance had come their way. But, being England, those chances were severely restricted, denied and delayed – to be conceded, eventually with a great deal of foot-dragging and objection.

The pre-eminent school in Manchester was Manchester Grammar school (MGS), which drew boys from an enormous catchment area of the north west, and dispatched dozens of them each year to Oxford and Cambridge. It had a fierce reputation, and the rest of us – envious and generally in awe – lived under its shadow. We regarded MGS boys as very clever: some were of course, but many weren't, though we didn't realise it at the time. MGS pupils exuded a social confidence among themselves, and towards the world at large, that the rest of us lacked. That confidence and self-belief was one of those virtues which was cultivated by the High Master, Eric James. Unfortunately for many boys at Ducie, we shared many of the same bus routes heading to school. And it was there, on Manchester Corporation buses heading down Oxford Road, that we were exposed on a daily basis to MGS self-confidence and cleverness. I used to scrutinise MGS boys closely. Many of them seemed to read obscure texts en route to school, merely confirming my view that they were all brainy swots. The ultimate confirmation of their intellectual superiority came at a German O-level oral examination held in a Manchester University lecture hall in 1958.

Apart from two of us from Ducie, the room was packed with candidates from MGS. We were all supposed to comprehend and transcribe the German text read out loud to us, and then answer oral questions about it. At the coffee break, as the two of us from Ducie hovered nervously on the edge of the MGS mob, one of them proclaimed 'I thought his German was frightful!'. We could hardly believe our ears. For an hour, the two of us had toiled simply to understand what the speaker was saying. Now we learned, and from another schoolboy, that the examiner's German was bad. Even worse followed:

'Yes. I thought he had a really strong Swabian accent.'

My Ducie contemporary and I stared at each other in disbelief. ('Fuck me!' was the understated response of my partner in suffering.) What hope was there for us? How could we hope to compete with boys who could spot a German regional accent? The two of us took all this at its demoralising face value: yet another bunch of MGS clever boys and two dopes from Ducie.

I now suspect that it was simply cocky schoolboy bravado. It was, however, an early example of a phenomenon that I would become familiar with later: the use of assertive pretence in education. Say something with an air of confidence and social poise and people will believe you. It was to be a commonplace aspect of life in universities. Being surrounded by MGS boys in 1958 was my first lesson in the need for vigilance in sniffing out bullshit in the world of education.

★ ★ ★

By a fluke, I did well in my first school examinations at Ducie, and thereafter I resolved to repeat the pattern. I became an industrious little swot, keen not to be beaten in any subject, but especially, as I progressed through school, in the arts subjects I liked most. It seemed to work, and every year I won a prize for the best this or that. Though the school wasn't geared up for preparing boys for higher education, the headmaster, Sam Hughes, recognised that there were enough of us around with the potential to progress along academic paths. Along with a few others, I was also lucky to have masters who spotted our interests and talents, and who encouraged and helped, pushing us, lending us books, steering us in ways we needed, and generally instilling a confidence in our own abilities. The end result was that a small band of us thrived in the most unlikely of surroundings.

Sam Hughes managed an awkward school with a crisp officer-like presence. He got to know me initially because of my difficult domestic circumstances, but was quick to encourage my work. He lent me books (often on subjects I'd never dreamed about) and regularly took me aside to grill me about this and that. He was never too busy to offer a word of encouragement. Just as important, he exercised a humane common sense when my persistent domestic problems intruded on school work. Once, when Mum received a small pay rise, the extra income knocked me off the free school dinner list, and she was hence a few shillings worse off each week – no small matter at the time. Rather than battle with the bureaucracy of Manchester Education Authority, Sam simply ordered me to receive the free dinners allocated to an orthodox Jewish boy who brought kosher food from home (another revelation about life in Manchester – there were poor Jews!). No fuss or paperwork: just a simple, and absolutely sensible, headmasterly decision.

Primary school, of course, had been very local, with the children drawn from the immediate neighbourhood. Going to secondary school in Moss Side Manchester opened up a much wider range of school mates. There was, for example, a sizeable group of Jewish boys, largely from north Manchester, whose fathers were mainly in business, many of them in the rag trade. It was the first time I met people who weren't Christian. The prosperous Jewish boys were also the first people I got to know personally from middle-class homes. They were, of course, the object of much curiosity, teasing and open abuse:

'Who killed Christ?'

'It wasn't us. It was the Leeds Jews.'

Travelling to and from Moss Side between 1953 and 1960 effectively introduced me to the blackened panorama of Victorian Manchester, and prompted a growing curiosity about the city's history. It was a history that seemed to speak from its very fabric: its major buildings, memorials, banks, warehouses, factories, rail systems and canals – all monuments to the Victorian age. But what about the years *before* the rise of industry? And what about the story of the city's inhabitants? Some historical episodes of local history were obvious. The impact of the great wars, for example, was clear enough, in the persons of the men I'd grown to know, and in the ubiquitous war memorials and bomb sites. What really puzzled me, however, was a largely unrecognised history: the history of the working people who made up the community I was born into. In my years at Ducie I attended history lessons and read history books on a more or less daily basis, but I read or heard *nothing* about them. Treaties and dynastic matters, governors and kings passed in a seamless historical parade of the good and the great. But never an *ordinary* person, nothing about their lives and pleasures.

Yet the Manchester I travelled through and increasingly explored was manifestly the creation of generations of ordinary people, scurrying to and from their workplaces, called to arms periodically, worshipping in a variety of churches and chapels, and enjoying themselves at weekends and on summer breaks. Yet none of this – not so much as a passing mention – appeared, in lessons, in text books, or in the dozens of essays we had to write. Nothing I learned from the formal instruction in history seemed to address the world I belonged to. I was both fascinated and frustrated by the history I studied, keen to pursue it, but at the same time irritated by much of what we studied – or rather didn't study. There had to be someone, somewhere, addressing these issues.

The end result was that, for all the hours and days I spent in the formal study of history, my real historical curiosity was sparked, not by lessons or books, but by old people around me, especially the soldiers of the world wars – and by simply pounding the streets of Manchester.

★ ★ ★

School taught a range of formal topics, from knitting in primary school to woodwork and metalwork at Ducie. But the one subject that wasn't taught was sex. I learned how to join pieces of wood together, how to weld, and I even knew the details of the 1697 Treaty of Ryswick, but we learned nothing whatsoever about human biology and reproduction. Sex education was non-existent. To compound our ignorance, after the age of 11 (in another bizarre twist to English education) most of us lived in a highly segregated world. It was not usual for girls and boys to mix at secondary school. Until the drift toward co-education in the 1960s, boys and girls were generally herded into separate schools. Ducie was divided into two fiercely separated schools. In case we didn't grasp the principle, we were segregated by uncrossable thick white lines painted in the playground and up the stairs. Boys resided on one side, and on the ground floor, girls on the other side and upstairs. There was no mixing whatsoever in the building itself, in the playground, nor when travelling to and from school. Despite their physical proximity, girls were in effect a remote species, kept in enforced isolation. Naturally enough, the higher pitched gaggles of girls playing next door acted like a siren call to bolder spirits. Daring boys tried to make contact across the painted divide, and hoped that the supervising teachers wouldn't notice. Those who transgressed – by even so much as putting a foot over the line – were inevitably spotted and punished. This strictly enforced segregation merely exacerbated our natural and endless curiosity about girls.

Despite the fact that there were girls everywhere – at school, next door, in the neighbourhood – most of my mates and myself remained profoundly ignorant, well into our teens, about what made them different. Female anatomy was a source of endless curiosity and discussion but it was largely an area of complete ignorance, brightened by bizarre mythology. At primary school a friend had told us that menstruation started when a girl's penis dropped off. For a while we believed him. Boys with sisters told us about what they had seen. The primary school playground was sometimes a hotbed of lewd rumours, curiously about particular film stars. Everyone in my primary class seemed to know that Victor Mature and Errol Flynn both had unusually big penises, and as a result both men proved utterly irresistible to dozen of Hollywood's females. We all nodded our tiny heads in agreement when such stories were trotted out in the playground: all convinced that we were discussing widely known *facts*. No one ever asked the most obvious of questions: how did such an arcane matter become common knowledge in a Failsworth playground?

The more worldly wise told us stories about adult sexual activities they had encountered. A boy whose parents rented a holiday caravan told implausible tales about the vehicle mysteriously bouncing and rocking at night, even though there was no wind about. Such stories seemed so fantastic, so utterly unbelievable, that they might as well have been talking about the man in the moon. Until well into our teens, we talked about sex in a completely ignorant and ill-informed fashion. There was little to set against childhood and early teenage rumours and playground gossip, no formal instruction at primary or secondary school or at home. Fifty years later, my own grandson returned from school, aged nine, with enough biological detail about reproduction to qualify for medical school, courtesy of formal classroom instruction. We received nothing. Not a word. A few sensible parents took their children aside to talk about such matters, but they were utterly exceptional. And in any case, when they passed on what they had been told we tended not to believe it. Our own theories and speculations were much more interesting. Most of us wallowed in total ignorance about sex, and hence much of what we believed and what we discussed was usually wacky. What we knew was largely wrong, and what we whispered about was mainly bizarre. Even when we advanced into our teens, the early sexual experiences of our most precocious friends turned out to have been no less fanciful: adolescent boastings that impressed the rest of us only because we were utterly ignorant of the reality.

In our early teens we began to notice more open signs of adult sexuality, though again, they too were usually shrouded in mythology. We learned of certain places in Manchester where women walked up and down all day, small tell-tale chains round their ankles which broadcast to the world that they were prepared to have sex for a price. They also tended to like thick red lipstick (hard luck of course for other women who simply liked vivid lipstick). Lewis's Arcade was their favourite parade ground in the city centre. Others hovered on the corner, near our school

128

in Moss Side. Boys were also generally aware that barbers sold things to married men, for the weekend, which had something to do with sex. But exactly what, why and how, remained yet another elusive mystery. For all this gossip and rumour, much of what we learned did not exactly encourage us to look forward to sex. A lot of the rumours suggested that sex often led to widespread misery: women with unwanted babies, young men who lost their sight from unspeakable sexual activities, hair that mysteriously grew from the palm of the hand, ghastly diseases contracted from bizarre sexual habits – the dangers to body and mind were legion if you indulged in sex. Quite apart from the excruciating pain, madness and incapacity involved, sex could bring lasting shame on your whole family. In the face of such a barrage of misery, I often wondered why anyone bothered doing it in the first place.

Precisely *what* happened however – how to do it – remained as big a mystery as nuclear physics. Any questions or signs of curiosity were promptly brushed aside, silenced by a brusque (and generally embarrassed) dismissal. Reality came late, creeping slowly over the horizon as we headed through our teens. Men only a few months older than myself, swept up into the military for National Service, came home on leave with tales of sexual pleasures mixed with horror. They told of army induction films about sexual diseases, and – even worse – accounts of how army medics dealt with sexual disease. Apparently they pushed an umbrella-like contraption down your penis, opened it up, then drew it out, thus removing infection while inflicting maximum pain (and remorse) on the afflicted soldier. Yet these same young soldiers – the *Virgin Soldiers* of the later novel – also boasted of sexual encounters, most of them 'abroad' and therefore of the most spectacularly exotic variety. No one seemed prepared to admit to having had 'normal' local sex, though I had no real idea what that involved anyway. It always seemed to take place in Germany and Holland, in Malaya or Hong Kong. Until that is, the first boy in our group returned one night from Yates Wine Lodge in Oldham with a vivid account of his first experience of sexual bliss. We were all left agog at the details.

John was drinking, underage of course, and struck up a conversation, or so he said, with an older woman. Flushed by a schooner or two of Yates's finest, they embarked on a night of sexual abandon during which she accommodated him lavishly, using all her sexual experience and know-how to provide an initiation of dazzling complexity. A few days later, he provided us – spell-bound throughout – with lavish anatomical details. The trouble was, as I realised about 25 years later (when the memory unaccountably drifted back into focus) it simply could not have happened as he described it. His story was clearly a whopper on an epic scale. We should all have spotted the obvious biological flaws immediately, but none of us had the slightest idea of the reality, and therefore had nothing to compare his story to. We took his account of a first sexual encounter at eye-popping face value. His story was clearly a hilarious fib which no modern Western teenager would believe for a second. But, innocents in an age of innocence, we simply believed what we heard.

On this, as on many other things, I settled the matter in the Central Library. Round the corner from my favourite seat lurked the medical section, crammed with basic texts for medical students and anyone else (like myself) keen to know more about how we all functioned. At first I felt much as I had when peeking at the seaside postcards behind my mother's back a decade before. *Gray's Anatomy* and related texts sorted out a host of misunderstandings. But that was still a long way removed from the warm presence of a female body. Still, between the Library, Sunday School dance classes and an emergent common sense, I was happy enough. Others found their way towards adult life in their own stumbling fashion, but even so, on the eve of going to university, many – perhaps most of us – remained astonishingly ignorant about the realities of sex. Those who knew the truth sensibly kept it to themselves; those who didn't continued to flounder in make-believe, their heads filled with fantasy and unrequited lust. Here was a perfect example of the fact that the past – and the recent past at that – is not so much a foreign country as a distant galaxy.

★ ★ ★

By the age of 16 I had come to take Manchester's Central Library for granted. I owned few books of my own, but I felt I didn't need to: they were all available in the library. It was always open whenever I needed to study, and there I found everything I needed and more besides. But mine wasn't that autodidactic route beloved of romantics' views of nineteenth- and twentieth-century social life. Throughout I was nudged and prompted in the right direction by a handful of committed teachers. Because the sixth form was such a small group, we got their close attention. Their help, and being guinea-pigs in the launch of General Studies A level, also widened my intellectual interests. That innovation was an attempt to broaden the intellectual horizons of sixth formers, most of whom, even at 16, were already far too specialised and concentrated in their favourite subjects. With no formal syllabus, the course was, predictably enough, instantly attacked by myopic critics and by proponents of traditional disciplines. The new course was, however, just what I needed, allowing us to range far and wide. It fired my curiosity, though again with the help of a fine teacher.

Thus between 1958 and 1960, and partly because of this new area of study, I found myself drawn to the remarkable upsurge of interest in the very world I had grown up in. As we argued about the various studies of contemporary British life – Hoggart above all others – and tried to make sense of the cultural trends around us, it became apparent that there *were* means and ways of studying and understanding the history of life in Manchester, and even in Failsworth. I was equally clear, however, that my own curiosity and understanding were not being fed by historians. The writers and scholars who were raising major questions about contemporary issues were sociologists, playwrights, novelists and literary critics. The only historians I encountered, and the ones I studied, seemed to be living the lives of medieval strip farmers: up and down the same narrow strip of land, year after year, happy and contented in themselves, but unavailable to comment on the problems we struggled with, even though those problems had historical roots. Historians were notable by their absence from the exciting cultural debates of the late 1950s. Even so, I retained a zeal for studying history and hoped that, somehow, it could be turned to good effect. I had to wait until 1963, and the publication of E. P. Thompson's *The Making of the English Working Class*, before I found exactly what I was looking for.

Richard Hoggart tended to dominate our discussions, but he was just one actor in a crowded cast of commentators about the current state of British learning and culture. Print journalism and the airwaves fairly buzzed with debate about the state of current British culture. There was, of course, a kaleidoscope of views, but they tended to coalesce into two sides. Influenced by my special interest in the French Revolution at school I began to think of the cultural debates in 1958–60 as much like France in 1789. The British cultural *ancien régime* put up a dogged defence of the status quo. But the other side was winning.

The old guard was particularly opposed to new forms of culture – popular culture – notably music but above all television, especially after the advent of commercial television in 1955. They defended old habits and ingrained customs almost as if they were besieged by alien forces – which, after a fashion, they were. They were deeply concerned, alarmed even, about new cultural forces lapping against their battlements. The redoubts of the grammar schools were under attack, TV was eating into the foundations of high culture, and – this, one of Hoggart's prime concerns – printed ephemera (magazines, comics, cheap novels) were apparently corroding serious literature. All this is a great simplification of course, but in my late teenage eyes there seemed to be two major forces locked in cultural combat: a popular culture (with much deeper roots than its opponents allowed) and a resistant old order anxious to repel all new comers. The debate – the clash – wasn't new, of course. Similar arguments had thrived a century before. But the late 1950s witnessed the polarising of opinion into a tug of war for the cultural soul of Britain. What was it going to be? Bill Haley or Barbirolli? *The Brains Trust* or ITV? From the first I thought much of the debate oddly unnecessary. Why did it have to be one or the other? Why couldn't we settle for a new kind of cultural pluralism that allowed people to pick and choose as they saw fit. Was it so odd to like the Hallé *and* Manchester United?

The confusion was made worse by the fact that the whole debate, which touched most areas of contemporary British life, came wrapped in distinctive British social snobberies. There was disdain about the spread of new material prosperity: scoffing remarks when poorer sorts began to enjoy things previously beyond their reach. You didn't need to be a scholar to see that at the heart of the discussion there simmered a growing unease about the cracks in the world of social deference. Large numbers of people were getting above themselves.

All this made for an intellectually exciting time to be a young adult, though I now realise that I was too focused, too constrained, to enjoy it fully. I knew what I wanted – to go to university – and felt that everything else must be relegated to that end. To achieve that, I needed Manchester Central Library, and the peace and quiet of Joe Eyre's front room.

CHAPTER 10

Abroad

We knew plenty of people who had travelled abroad, but they were all ex-military who had been shipped to various theatres of war. Not surprisingly perhaps, they had little positive to say about 'abroad'. I grew up listening to their complaints: the tropics involved sapping heat, dangerous bugs and venomous bites; the desert meant unrelenting daytime heat, cold nights and flies; and France meant – well, France. Fred Ogden in Mesopotamia (Iraq), men from the North African campaign, Joe Eyre in Malaya and Japan, and Stanley of course in France, all had negative experiences. They trotted out tales which had different geographies but all culminated in similar denunciations, and produced a cartoon view of the world at large: dangerous locations, untrustworthy foreigners, foul local weather, unspeakable food. Their views, and their accounts of distant places, could have been culled directly from any popular boys' comic at any date from 1900 onwards. It would be wrong though to dismiss such caricatured views merely as the results of popular cheap publications. There were deep-seated racial and jingoistic attitudes that were succoured and maintained in the press, in politics and through formal schooling.

It was no surprise to know that such views were common, even vociferous, among people who had never left Britain. Everyone knew that abroad was beastly, and you had no need to travel abroad to believe it. Even Americans – millions of them familiar as recent guests in Britain during the war itself – were suspect, largely because of their brashness and their superior material wellbeing. Joe Eyre was dismissive of the US Navy because the ship transporting him from Manila to San Francisco offered men a choice of ice cream at meal times: 'What sort of Navy does that?'

This general dislike of the outside world and its inhabitants was set against a universal pride in the simple facts of a benign British imperial story. At its most obvious in the maps on our classroom walls, proclaiming vast stretches of the world as an imperial pink or red (i.e. ours), the attachment to empire seemed to have embedded itself deep in most people's brains. Empire was a matter of pride – an achievement unmatched in human history. We now know how this sense of superiority was cultivated, partly deliberately, but in the main by an accidental *ad hoc* brew of religious, political and cultural elements.

I thank the goodness and the grace
That on my birth has smiled,
And made me, in these Christian days,
A happy English child.

Many different influences had combined to create a remarkably potent and widespread attachment to the British empire: compulsory education from the 1880s on, especially the teaching of history and geography, and the powerful influence of print and of popular culture, reaching back to the great days of the Music Hall, and particularly the songs and verses of imperial triumphs and splendours. And this attachment included a loyalty to the monarchy which sat astride this massive imperial enterprise.

How happy is our lot
Who live on Britain's isle!
Which is of heaven the favour'd spot,
Where countless blessings smile.

We regularly used the curious generic word 'foreigners' to dismiss anyone who wasn't British. There were even lots of 'foreigners' close to hand. The Irish, of course, occupied their own special position. Not exactly foreign, but certainly alien and strange, largely, in our eyes, because of their religion. We even recited a vulgar local folk rhyme about an IRA man hanged in the 1920s:

Old MacSweeney's dead and gone.
We won't see him no more.
Someone's pinched his coffin lid
To make a shithouse door.

Jews too flitted in and out of this demonology. Local, or just down the road, they were strange and distant. Needless to say, they were the object of a pervasive gut dislike – an anti-Semitism that ran naturally and unchallenged through English veins.

We had plenty of Americans to gaze at, and admire or envy. Lots of American servicemen passed in and out of local homes and Blackpool boarding houses, but we also saw lonely GIs on dates with local women. I only picked up the hints of the sexual jealousy involved much later. One of the first dirty jokes I heard as a schoolboy was about Americans. 'How can you tell a pair of wartime 'utility' knickers? One Yank and they're off.' Much less at ease in our neighbourhood were the gangs of miserable-looking Italian POWs, billeted in a disused factory just round the corner from my home, again with the attendant friction caused when they dated local women. I heard a post-war boast that one of them had been thrown into the Rochdale Canal simply for courting a local woman. Soon after the war ended, large numbers of refugee Poles, imported to work in the cotton mills, appeared in Oldham. One Polish woman – I only knew her as Jean – was taken up by my welcoming grandparents, and struggled to explain, in her faltering English, how hideous the war had been. Her suffering must indeed have been terrible, because she loved my grandmother's cooking and dined with us on Sunday as if at a state banquet.

Above all, Germany and Germans occupied their own special niche in the demonology of foreigners. The war and the incessant wartime propaganda generated widespread anti-German anger that lingered on long after hostilities ended. Even men chastened by the sights of a devastated post-war Germany (my Uncle Jack Wood was one) found it hard to forgive Germany for creating such widespread suffering – *again*. As if that were not enough, as if any doubts still lingered about the war, vans toured the town shortly after the war showing films of the liberated concentration camps. Locals stumbled away from the films feeling that the war had, after all, been worthwhile. But it was clearly going to be a long time before reconciliation settled among us. I had no sense of similar views towards the Japanese, except for those who, like Joe, had suffered directly. It was, as he and others complained, the forgotten war.

In the wake of this confused mix of attitudes to the wider world, it was hardly surprisingly that there was little to recommend 'abroad' and the people who lived there.

I recognise that I was as influenced as anyone else around me by this crude mix of prejudices about the wider world. Better to stick with what we knew: bankrupt, beaten-up, meagrely rationed Britain. Those, like my Uncle Jack Walvin, who found that prospect too depressing, emigrated. But then, quite suddenly, in 1956, all that changed for me. That summer I began to look at the world in a very different light. It was a fundamental change brought about by an experience which, today, seems so ordinary, so routine, that it might even pass unremarked. That July, I went abroad for the first time to spend a month with a French family.

My French baptism took place, suitably, on Bastille Day in Tours, though the national celebrations that year were muted on government orders. The country seemed hopelessly mired in the sufferings of the Algerian war, and excessive French pleasures at home were thought inappropriate. That, alongside the call '*buvez du lait*' (Pierre Mendès France's plea to drink milk instead of wine – a lost cause if ever there was one) formed the unusual and low-key background to what should have been traditional mid-summer French revels. This general political gloom in France had no impact on me, and despite all the cultural baggage I carried with me, I was hooked. Hooked from the first sight of France as the ferry drifted into its Boulogne moorings, from that first distinctive smell that was France, and from the moment the first porter came on board, all blue dungarees, beret, a dead Gauloises stuck to his lips, stepping among the arriving passengers in search of trade. I was instantly smitten by France: the beginnings of a lifelong love affair.

It is hard, now, to convey how different France was in almost every respect, from everything I knew and recognised. It was also utterly removed from the France I'd heard about from Stanley and others, and I was completely unprepared for what I encountered that summer. But the impact of France went far beyond learning about France itself, and involved much more than a schoolboy's discovery of a new country. France brought with it a new recognition about my own homeland – even about myself. When viewed from my temporary perch in France that summer, a visit of one month in the Loire Valley, England itself looked different. When I thought about England, the north, Manchester, they all seemed very different from the other side of the Channel. That month in France was a time of pleasurable but fundamental change: my head filled with Frenchness. First, the wrestling with schoolboy French, and coming to terms with the domestic lives of ordinary French working people, most strikingly eating good simple food for the first time, even the new delight of sipping (diluted) local wine. Then there was France itself (or my corner of it) and exploring the Loire Valley by bike and camping. France turned my head and filled it with a seductive confusion of all things French. I returned home (my French friend Claude in tow) awash with French ideas, and generally brimming with what must have seemed French contrariness.

It took a long time to realise that I returned home a changed person. Now I spouted praise left and right for all things French. I talked about it to family, friends and school mates. Most of them remained unimpressed and, if they responded at all, were content to fall back on the timeless English contempt for France and its inhabitants. But my new-found interest was to have some unexpected consequences. It was precisely after I came home from France, and in response to my enthusiastic Francophilia, that the veterans I knew from both world wars began to open up about their wars. In a curious and unpredictable way, my endless babble about France seemed to break the seal. The summer of 1956 left me nursing a Gallic bug, and in response to my daily praise for France, Stanley began to talk about the trenches, and Joe, quietly bored by my endless chirping about France, talked for the first time about other more distant and more exotic foreign countries, and how horrible they all were – all of them. Quite unconsciously, and unknown to each other, both men came together to counter my admiration for France by echoing the English doctrine that 'abroad is beastly'.I had to admit that in both cases, it was true that their lives abroad had been beastly beyond words.

★ ★ ★

I lived in a community where most of the men and youths did manly physical work, but I remained a bookish schoolboy, with my nose glued to books at home and in Manchester Central Library. In the autumn of 1956 I must also have become an irritating adolescent challenge to relatives and friends, not merely because of normal teenage awkwardness, but through my inquisitive and doubting presence. Relatives clearly found my ideas and questions 'half-baked' (their favourite word for stupid) and all acquired, they thought, either by reading too much or, more directly, by 'letting France go to your head' – my mother's way of dismissing my new habit of querying life at large. After a fashion, she was correct. It was as if France had helped the scales fall from my very English eyes. For that I owe a debt to Froggy.

Mr Hulme the French master, known as Froggy, was English, but he appeared every bit a French bourgeois: beret, baggy double-breasted suits, proudly sporting the ribbon of a French state honour on the lapel. He worked tirelessly, though chaotically, to promote France and to inculcate a love of French and France into groups of largely indifferent Manchester schoolboys. He also ran a brilliant exchange scheme, and in 1956 he asked if I was interested in spending time with a French family (I'd proved myself competent in his French classes). On the pretext of persuading my mother to agree, he visited our house with a suitcase full of cuttings, pictures and maps. In reality he came to case the joint: did he really want to dispatch a young French boy to our house, and others like it? Despite our limitations we evidently passed the test, and on 13 July 1956 Mr Hulme, along with a gaggle of adolescents (including me, armed with £5 to last for the month) left Manchester for the Gare du Nord. There he transferred his apprehensive brood to various French parents who had descended on Paris from across France to collect their English visitors. I was introduced to yet another classic Frenchman, M. Bonamie – another beret, more Gauloises, and a warm, calloused-handed welcome – and we were off, travelling south-west to Tours.

Mr Hulme's great skill lay in getting the pairings right and matching families with appropriate guests and hosts. The Bonamies were ordinary working people; the father worked for SNCF and the mother was an attendant at a local swimming pool. Their house on the edge of Tours was fairly rustic, and the outside old-fashioned squatting lav added to my initial confusion. But what totally floored me was the food and dining. A series of small dishes, many of them containing home-grown produce, all simply and deliciously cooked, all neatly served, and every one with a glass of wine (watered in my case). At first I felt confused, but quickly got into my French stride, settling into what quickly became a wonderful summer, with long bike rides around the Loire valley, from Villandry to Chenonceaux and Blois, plus camping on the Atlantic coast (using free train tickets thanks to M. Bonamie's job on the railways). I grew ever more confident with simple spoken French, to the extent that by the end of the trip (though I now cringe to think of it) at a family wedding, a glass of Vouvray emboldened me to propose a toast to the *entente cordiale*. The boozy smoky wedding party applauded furiously, and with approval: '*Bien fait, mon brave!*' It was my first speech in public, and remains, 60 years later, and despite hundreds in between, perhaps my best – certainly my bravest. Though the diluted Vouvray helped.

Exploring the Loire Valley for a month was a very good idea. But what about the other side of the exchange? Why did Claude want to visit Manchester for a month? What we offered in return were pretty meagre pleasures. A life that was good enough and ample for our own purposes – but what did it hold for a young Frenchman? Take, for example, the food. Claude was driven to eat what was placed in front of him from sheer desperation, but he took to muttering, between mouthfuls of Spam and potatoes. Even the excursions and treats we offered must have seemed pretty sparse compared to the châteaux of the Loire. We went to watch Lancashire play Australia, and he sat uncomprehendingly throughout a whole day's play. We visited Blackpool, of course, and that too prompted a similar Gallic shrug. We were given a tour of a cotton mill by Grandpa Wood, but for all that, a trip to Manchester could hardly have seemed a fair exchange for a month in the Loire Valley. Finally Claude was gone and I was ready for a return to school.

★ ★ ★

Quite apart from going abroad for the first time, 1956 proved a good summer for me to develop a critical approach to Britain's dealings with the outside world. The early stages of the Suez Crisis unfolded when I was in France. Throughout the summer, as the crisis worsened following Nasser's nationalisation of the Suez Canal, the French and the British governments clearly planned to retaliate. I tried to follow events through French newspapers and my occasional access to English newspapers, but it was only when I was back at school, and when the crisis flared into disastrous military conflict in the autumn, that I became aware of the astonishing bitterness and divides laid bare by the Suez conflict.

I had, so far, only known my teachers in their various classroom modes: largely placid and professional. Now I saw them in an utterly different light: in their attitudes to Suez they revealed themselves as one small example of a British society greatly at odds with itself. The military action, the blatant complicity of the British, French and Israelis, the brazen lies involved and the eventual ignominious retreat (from Suez – and thence from empire) triggered ferocious arguments among the teaching staff. I had a bird's eye view of their fierce arguments because I had a lunchtime job setting up equipment in the chemistry labs, the very place where the staff took their lunch breaks. The raucous severity of the arguments about Suez amazed me, and exposed a side to the staff I'd never suspected. The all-male staff was riven by Suez, with lunchtime shouting and slanging matches of a kind I'd never seen before. I was so astonished and intrigued to see teachers bellowing at each other that I deliberately went slow, taking longer than necessary to set up the equipment, in order to witness the continuing daily arguments. And, in the heat of the moment, the combatants forgot that I was in the same room. At times I thought they might come to blows.

Many of the teachers were themselves World War II men, some of them still displaying in their posture and style the traces of five years of military life. None more so than Mr Lee, my history master, who ran his classes like an infantry platoon. I didn't much like his style of teaching: he simply dictated, and we took down notes, and were only expected to open a book and speak when the class was over. Curiously though, it whetted my appetite for more. Mr Lee was famed and feared as a severe martinet whose word was heeded and never challenged. He looked, walked (or marched really), dressed and behaved for all the world like an ex-soldier, though more RSM than officer. Most of the time he was a restrained and apparently self-controlled man. Now, in the autumn of 1956, I saw him shouting at the top of his voice about Suez. Mr James, a chemistry teacher, was so angry he turned red in the face. The row became so intense that the headmaster, Sam Hughes, intervened to calm things down. Sam was a man from a humble Yorkshire background, with an Oxford history degree and a record as a devoted and excellent schoolmaster. He too had been in combat from Normandy to Germany, and now brought some of his officer qualities to bear, striding into the chemistry lab to impose tranquillity when the argument had reached such a pitch that he could hear it in his distant office. Sam spotted me and, sensibly, ordered me out, away from the spectacle of such unseemly anger among his staff. I had never before, and have rarely since, seen such public political anger. It was obvious even to a naïve schoolboy that what I had witnessed was merely a local example of the sharp divisions and passions generated by Suez throughout the country.

Though my schoolmasters were at each other's throats about Suez, at home and among neighbours most of this went largely unnoticed and unremarked, except for the usual derogatory comments about Egypt and Egyptians. The universal dislike of Arabs was a by-product, I think, of the time many local men had served in North Africa, returning home with a visceral distaste for all things Arabic. Long before Suez, I had regularly heard Arabs denounced as a bunch of untrustworthy mendacious thieves. It was an attitude that took firm root among the public at large and, once again, it raised a baffling puzzle which I found very hard to explain. People I knew who had little to show for a lifetime's toil, and who were themselves condescended to in their own country, none the less felt superior and dismissive of others about whom they knew virtually nothing. I was genuinely confused by what I could see and hear around me. What made the British – of all sorts and conditions – feel so much superior to the rest? I had returned home from France that summer especially puzzled by why the British held the French in such low esteem – 'dirty buggers' in Stanley's oft-repeated characterisation. Though Stanley's antipathy was historical, born and nurtured by life on the Western Front, it was widely shared, certainly by all my relatives, not one of whom had crossed the Channel. How could this welter of hostility to outsiders be explained? Perhaps all this had historical roots and perhaps the explanation lay in Britain's historical past? It wasn't clear at the time, but it now seems obvious: events were pushing me towards a more serious study of history.

CHAPTER 11

The People's Game

It was late afternoon, 6 February 1958 and we were heading into Manchester on the school bus when we saw the first newspaper placards:

UNITED PLANE CRASH. MANY DEAD.

We joined the growing crowds gathering around the news vendors in the city centre. The first reports gave the broad outlines and the details followed over the next few hours. The plane carrying the Manchester United team back from Belgrade had crashed on take-off on an icy runway at Munich. The final death toll was 23, with a long list of seriously injured. It was one of those 'tell-me-it-isn't-true' moments. The club that Alan and I had followed avidly, the club Dad had followed as a boy, and which Grandpa Wood had watched at the 1909 Cup Final lay shattered, seemingly beyond repair.

★ ★ ★

Watching and playing football was a source of endless boyhood fun (and occasionally gloom) from one year to another. There was never any doubt that Alan and I would support Manchester United. Like millions of fans with their favourite teams, we had no choice in the matter. We were simply born into it. Dad had been a United fan from his boyhood, and we grew up in a house where Manchester United was revered. As boys we played football whenever we could. The game's universal charm – then as now – was its simplicity. You could play it anywhere, on fields or in back alleys. A single child can play alone, kicking a ball against a wall. But with two coats or pullovers as goalposts and the company of three or four mates, you have a game. As boys we played it everywhere – in the fields behind the house, in local alleys, on patches of spare land, against any available wall. Boys would turn up, lingering on the edge of the game, waiting to be asked to join in or simply entering the game uninvited. Our favourite gift at Christmas was *The FA Book for Boys*, and apart from bikes (bought one year by an uncle) the most prized gift we received was a pair of leather football boots, though they were clumsy clunky objects, and a real leather football, along with the dubbin to keep everything in good condition. Though I tried to reserve my precious boots and the football for games on grass, inevitably we were drawn into kickabouts on spare land, on cinder tracks, against a neighbour's wall (to their intense irritation) – anywhere in fact that provided space for a game.

My enthusiasm for football, however, was not matched by any skill. In fact I was a hopeless footballer. I could never decide: was I worse at football or dancing? I was slow, had no real ball skills, and not much stamina for the game's rough and tumble. Being small was a disadvantage among growing and boisterous boys and I was easily elbowed aside. The end of my playing days was in sight when, as a student, I played against a team from the Potteries bus company. A large bus driver – a total stranger – whispered to me as we lined up at the kick off, 'I'll get you, you little twat'. And he did. After that I much preferred to be a spectator.

Despite my athletic shortcomings, I loved the game, and assumed that all boys felt the same way. On this, as with many other things, university provided a rude awakening. I made friends who were indifferent to the game, and some even looked down their noses at it. But all that was to come. For now, football was a family inheritance and a boyhood passion, played whenever there was enough light. Best of all – better even than playing or talking about football – we had Manchester United.

Grandpa Wood enjoyed both football and Rugby League, and seemed more attracted to Oldham Athletic (whose ground was close to our grandparents' home) than to Manchester United and he regularly took me as a small boy to watch Oldham. One of my first and most vivid memories of watching Oldham is of a small inoffensive-looking older fan who stood close to us: amiable and chatty before the game, he directed regular and filthy abuse at whichever innocent linesman was trotting along the touchline. Every game, he bellowed his favourite refrain, and always prompted by the most trivial of decisions: 'Linesman! Stick your head down t'shithouse hole!'. That was my first real encounter with raw adult vulgarity, and with football's amazing ability to transform normal folk into demented ranters.

In his own pre-1914 youth, Grandpa Wood had followed United, and had even travelled to the 1909 Cup Final at Crystal Palace – 10/6d (52½p) return from Oldham Mumps station. My own boyhood enthusiasm for United, especially when I began to gush about the 'Busby Babes', and my own hero, Duncan Edwards, made Grandpa nostalgic about football's golden days before 1914. He was especially prone to pontificate about United's 1909 half-back line: 'Duckworth, Roberts and Bell. T'finest half-back line tha's ever seen.'

Spoken 50 years after the 1909 Final, Grandpa's praise failed to impress me, just as, another half century later, my own eloquence about the 1958 United team failed to impress my own grandson. By then, a century after the 1909 Final, there had been five generations of Manchester United fans in the family: my grandfather, my Dad, myself and Alan, our sons and my grandson. It is a family trait that some find hard to fathom.

If anyone was to blame for the family's United bug it was our father. Family legend had it that his first date with Mum had been to watch United. It poured down, they were soaked, and United lost 4–0 to Derby. Afterwards he was miserable and refused to talk to her for the entire evening (he clearly had a way with women).Though he was too sick to take us to watch United regularly, we gossiped endlessly about them. Even as he grew sicker, and was confined to bed for long periods, United's current state was a regular bedside topic. During the working week there was even a 7 a.m. clarion call of 'Up the Reds!' shouted up to his bedroom window by a mate walking to work at the rubber factory at the end of the road. That regular call became a family mantra: a simple and oft-repeated declaration of passion for the club. It was simply inevitable that Alan and I would follow suit.

Before the coming of televised football, we listened to the radio for Saturday's results, and read the Saturday evening football special, 'The Pink'. I loved the 5 p.m. theme tune for *Sports Report*, heralding those tense few moments as results were announced, with the broadcaster's intonation of early scores (the way he placed different emphases on the home and visitor's scores) perhaps giving a clue to what United's result might be. The first game I heard live on the radio was the 1948 Cup Final (United beat Blackpool 4–2) which I listened to huddled close to the radio with my father. The first live game I watched, again in 1948, was United playing Manchester City at Maine Road. Old Trafford had been bombed and United played all their home games at City's ground until 1949. I can recall only a few snapshots of the game: of being perched on an adult's shoulders in a vast swaying crowd before being passed overhead towards the front. Along with dozens of other small children, I was seated on the running track behind City's goal, awe-struck as their large goalie, Frank Swift, picked up the ball in one of his large mitts. A man who could pick up a football with one hand – a giant! Even those vague, distant memories capture many of the game's enduring spectator appeal: the noise, the crowd itself, the pungent smell of the players' liniment, all the boisterous, raucous, intensity – adding up to an excitement of a kind I've never found anywhere else. The game had its downside of course. As for Dad on his first date with Mum, when United lost, Saturday evening could be dull and miserable. Non-fans simply don't get it; football fans know it all too well.

When Alan and I were very young, we went to games in the care of friendly adults. Later we travelled to football grounds around the country – from Workington to Norwich – courtesy of British Rail 'football specials' and local motor coaches. As we got older we ventured out and about on our own, with me in charge. Alan carried an old school hand-bell to wave in support. Until that is, the 1957 Semi-final played at Hillsborough, Sheffield. We were wedged in the middle of a tightly packed crowd and Alan's bell suddenly stopped clanging: the clapper had flown out into the crowd. It *must* have hurt someone, and

Alan hurriedly hid the bell before anyone could trace the person responsible for firing a metal clapper into a dense crowd.

I loved the excitement and the camaraderie of the games, especially the barmy joshing and joking, and the funny vulgarities (not to be repeated at home, or anywhere else for that matter) which were flung at opposing players and officials. It was a basic earthy kind of pleasure. Even so, it came with its limitations. The stadiums were run-down and poorly equipped. The swaying back and forth in a packed crowd often felt dangerous. Worst of all was the habit of men, fresh from the pub, peeing on the crowded terraces (through a newspaper rolled into a cone to avoid collateral splashing). I was once hit by a hot meat pie at Goodison Park, to my mother's immense irritation when she saw the resulting grease marks on my raincoat. For all that, the atmosphere on those unreformed grounds, especially when United won, more than compensated: the noise and the fun, the earthy smells of a large good-natured crowd, the half-time refreshments (unspeakable pies and Bovril), the journeys far afield (twice to London to watch the Cup Final) – all this in addition to the thrilling uncertainty and excitement of the matches.

* * *

The club we watched as schoolboys was transformed in 1957 when Matt Busby created a new kind of team, built around a group of very young players. They quickly settled into a dazzling youthful team destined to achieve great things. Even the most gnarled and jaundiced of newspaper hacks were impressed. And from 1957 they could test themselves against the best in Europe. Until then, English football had been remarkably insular – local even. Rivalries were defined almost along parochial lines:

City or United, Liverpool or Everton, Spurs or Arsenal. All the major teams I saw as a boy were English, large numbers of them from the north-west, though most had a sprinkling of Irish and Scottish players and managers. In 1957 however, the game began to look to Europe for a new kind of challenge.

Planes began to deliver what seemed to us to be exotic teams from all corners of Europe to play in Manchester in the European Cup. Teams from Belgium and Spain, Yugoslavia, Czechoslovakia and Germany turned out on grey mid-week Manchester nights, bringing with them a sporting exoticism which was utterly unfamiliar. Today it is unremarkable; then it was new and exciting. Even the discordant efforts of the Beswick Prize Band (the standard pre-match and half-time entertainment at Old Trafford), now struggling to master the Yugoslav national anthem for example, couldn't take the gloss off those early European football nights in Manchester.

Not all the visiting teams were brilliant (we beat most of them) but the best – Real Madrid – were sensational. For a start they looked different. They seemed sleeker than our players. Their all-white kit was neat and trim where ours was baggy; their boots looked more like velvet carpet slippers while ours were – well, boots. They appeared to stroll through a game where even our young players puffed and hurried. Real Madrid played with an effortless grace, and always seemed to have time on their side. Of course Madrid boasted some of the greatest players of that generation: wonderful footballers who were drawn from across Europe and South America, but they had the knack of making the most dazzling play look easy, and the most brilliant goals look simple. When we talked about them afterwards, we asked ourselves: were they playing a different game?

One of the surprises in France in 1956 had been to learn that the French also liked football. I arrived there convinced that the French sporting passion was only for cycling. But not only did they appear as keen on football as the British, but they had a *vision* for the game which was almost absent in Britain. The French appreciated the potential for European-wide football competitions at a time when the English were more likely to be arguing about the price of meat pies at half-time in Burnley. The European Cup – which had only vaguely caught my attention at that point – was a French invention, promoted by the French sports newspaper, *L'Équipe*, a sporting publication which had no comparable equivalent or rival in Britain.

This small and highly specialised world of European football reflected the wider story of European integration in the 1950s. Western Europe was drawing closer together, but the British languished, insular and sceptical, on the sidelines. Just as in the world of politics, those who advocated close links between British and European football had to battle against doggedly resistant and inward-looking British football authorities. What was wrong with the old game: of meat pies at half-time, in old stadiums and in competitions devised by Victorians? At football, as in politics and life in general, we were deeply un-European. Then, just as the English pioneers in the European game – Manchester United – were making a real impact, and opening people's eyes to the potential of the European game, everything crashed.

* * *

Though our school was very close to City's stadium at Maine Road, the boys at Ducie were fairly evenly divided between United and City. On 6 February 1958 those of us on the school bus were all stunned by the placards announcing the Munich crash, and we couldn't really believe what we read. There was a confused gabble and loud speculation about what it might mean, before we jumped off the school bus in Piccadilly. It soon became clear enough.

The impact of the Munich air crash on the city of Manchester that day was astonishing. By the time we arrived, about 4.30 p.m., the city centre was already filling with large groups of confused people, crowds spilling out of shops, offices and workplaces. Buildings simply emptied as thousands of people left their work and poured onto the streets, surrounding the nearest news vendors. There were no mobiles, no portable radios, no ubiquitous TV monitors – none of today's instant news information, no immediate contact with the outside world. Our access to news was via newspapers. *The Manchester Evening News* worked itself into a frenzy (reporters were among the dead and injured), their presses spitting out one edition after another, with each fresh bit of news from the wires, and phone calls from Munich immediately printed in the stop-press columns. Vans shuttled round the city, dropping off bundles of papers with the latest stop-press news. Vendors were immediately overwhelmed by a sea of waving arms as people grabbed the latest edition, before backing away with their copy, reading aloud the fudged details: so many dead, so many injured, others unaccounted for. For a couple of hours I shuffled from one seller to another in the centre of Piccadilly, waiting for the latest news, but when it became clear that further news would merely bring more of the same – a litany of disaster – I drifted home.

The huge industrial-commercial sprawl of Manchester effectively ground to a halt. Tens of thousands of people left their workplaces early, heading either for the news vendors or straight home to listen to the radio or watch TV. Word of mouth sent news and rumours spinning across the city. Fans of both Manchester teams, and legions of people who had no interest in the game or in the club, were drawn together in a mood of deep collective sorrow.

The end result is now familiar (and remains the essential background to the club's status). The Munich crash left 23 dead, eight of them players, and a host of others grievously injured. An exciting young team had been shattered beyond repair, and the club now lay broken-backed and grieving, along with the city at large. Older relatives later said that the sense of communal grief was greater even than it had been in the Blitz. For many days Manchester was a desolate place, its traditional flinty and chirpy self-confidence blown apart. The people I knew best, relatives and friends, were not given to public expressions of private feelings. Men in particular were likely to dismiss public tears and emotion as a sign of softness – being a 'mard-arse', to use the popular local phrase. But this time was different. It was another of those rare moments when I saw grown men weep, and shuffle off, drying their eyes.

A week later I went into Manchester late at night to watch the long cortège of hearses transport the bodies from the airport to Old Trafford. Despite the bad weather and the time (it was nearly midnight) huge crowds turned out to line the streets to pay their silent respects. The misery of it all lingered over the city like one of its infamous dark skies, and simply wouldn't go away. Over the coming weeks it was periodically revived, with each fresh bulletin: the progress of the injured, the news of their eventual crippled return to Manchester, and, worst of all, the late death of their greatest player, Duncan Edwards.

The sense of gloom, the depth of communal feeling that settled over Manchester, was tangible in February

1958 and is hard to convey half a century on. There was a collective outpouring of grief for the dead and the injured, but also a sense of general despair at the cruel dimming of young talent. As far as we knew, it meant a permanent stifling of one of the city's achievements, and an end to a source of pleasure for tens of thousands of people. It felt as if life had taken a turn for the worse.

It was an extraordinary moment in the city's history, and seems no less remarkable in retrospect. For the young people of my generation, who had not known the fears and the terrors faced by our parents and grandparents in two great wars, it was the worst of times, and we felt as if life would never be the same again. We were wrong, of course. Life revived and continued. Even United rose again – battered, patched up, carried along by a communal hysteria in their early games after the crash, and forever thereafter carrying the stigmata of a club once destroyed by a disaster, then rebuilt by its remarkable (but badly damaged) manager, Matt Busby.

That year, against the odds, United again made it to the Cup Final. Alan and I went, as we had to all the early rounds, and stood at Wembley to watch as a makeshift Manchester United team were, for the second year running, robbed – this time by Bolton Wanderers. It was to take until 1968 before Busby assembled yet another brilliant team which managed to do what his dead youth had failed to do a decade earlier and win the European Cup. By then, everything was very different: we were well on the way to being part of Europe.

★ ★ ★

Today I watch United's games live, in all corners of the world. If I can't get to a TV set, my brother Alan, long resident in Jakarta, calls or texts with the scores as the game progresses. In the face of the modern tidal wave of global football, it is hard to recapture the simple thrill of watching European football in its pioneering stages in the 1950s.

It is tempting to idealise the old game, and dismiss modern football as a sport corrupted by money. The differences in the professional game are, of course, staggering. In 1957 Alan and I waited for a bus after a game at Old Trafford next to our hero, Duncan Edward, his hair still wet from the shower after the game he'd just starred in. Here was the greatest player of his generation, queuing alongside the fans for a Manchester Corporation bus into the city. Today, if you walk past the players' car park at Old Trafford, you will find it ringed by razor wire and patrolled by security guards. Inside, a lavish collection of expensive cars gives the appearance of a glittering motor show.

For all that – the modern glitter, the multi-millionaire young footballers in fancy cars, the excess of television – football remains a simple game: the world's most enduring and popular game, played in all corners of the globe – in slums and alleyways in most of the world's massive cities. It remains today what it always was: the people's game. The same game I played so badly in my new pair of football boots in 1950.

CHAPTER 12

Better Times

If there was one dominant impulse in the house I grew up in, it was the commitment to hard work. This was understandable because we were raised by a woman who seemed to work endlessly: a variety of factory jobs, part-time jobs in the evenings and at weekends, and self-employed hair-dressing. She generated a pervasive culture of hard work – the sense almost that we were placed on earth solely to work – radiating a clear belief that if you wanted or needed anything you would have to work for it. This wasn't a philosophy or creed but merely a stark fact of local life, and the evidence was all around us. In a world of full employment, there was no shortage of casual, temporary and unskilled work, even for a part-time teenage worker like myself. When I came of working age at 15 I could even pick and choose between a variety of casual jobs.

My first paid work was the most traditional schoolboy job of a morning newspaper round. Even better, a local newsagent offered me the 6 a.m. round, which was better paid because of the early start and which suited my habit of rising early. I came to think of the job as stealing a march on the day. It was less attractive in winter and in Manchester's infamous rainy spells. Because the shop didn't provide waterproofs, rainy mornings inevitably involved a damp start and a hurried effort to dry myself before setting off, first with Ian to nursery, then to school in Manchester. It was hard to enjoy the job: there was too much donkey work – hauling and lifting a large heavy bag of newspapers. Trudging round the streets of Failsworth between 6 and 7 a.m. did not seem too unusual: there were lots of other people around heading to or from work. But the job also helped establish a pattern of work that became a permanent feature of my working life.

Each newspaper's destination was carefully numbered in pencil on the top right-hand corner, to ensure that the delivery boy pushed the paper through the appropriate letter box. Though I quickly learned to match papers with houses, mistakes invariably happened. Grumpy people, apparently lurking behind the front door at 6.30 a.m., ready to pounce on the paper, would call you back down the empty street if they received, say, the *Daily Herald* instead of the *News Chronicle*. A few were utterly miserable. One complained about my inveterate early morning whistling, and I was asked to desist. I stopped of course – at least outside their house – but thereafter I ensured that I periodically exposed their paper to the rain before placing the soggy issue through the letter box. 'That'll learn 'em!' was Grandma Wood's approving comment when I told her. However, such crabbiness was unusual, even at that early hour. Much more common were gruff greetings from my fellow early risers, heading to or from the factories or the bus stop.

Despite the early hour and the heavy loads, the job had two main attractions. First, I was able to read all the day's papers, scanning them quickly in the shop before and after my round, and pausing briefly, as I delivered them, to read the bits that caught my eye. Better still by far was the pay. Starting an hour before the other boys, I received a handsome 10 shillings (50p) for six mornings' work. It went straight into my new Post Office account, and slowly mounted to pay for my next trip to France. Periodically Mum had to borrow some, but I was always repaid. Today, the sums involved look unbelievably meagre. What once took me a year to save, I now spend, without giving it a second thought, on a book or a meal. But between 1957 and 1960 I looked on my Post Office account as a treasure which I hoarded to convert into a ticket to France and a bundle of French francs. Behind these commonplace and simple details lay something altogether more basic about the late 1950s: about working and saving money, and about the opening up of travel and 'abroad'.

I liked the idea of saving money in my very own Post Office account, and I wanted more. Uncle Joe stepped in and got me my first summer job working full time in the Failsworth hat factory. There, in 1957 and 1958, I was shuttled between various departments, wherever they needed a spare pair of hands. Though I was familiar with factory life through the lives and gossip of relatives and neighbours (Grandma Wood even took us into the mill so she could look after us as she worked), and you could see – and smell – factories from our front door, this was my first direct experience of working in a factory. Now I was a factory worker (of sorts) and keen to put the working world to rights. I was instantly struck by what looked like archaic ways of doing things. The whole process of making hats seemed riddled with old routines and peculiar working habits, all badly in need of a shake-up. Or so it seemed to a cocky 15 year old. For a short time, I wildly fancied myself as an apprentice time-and-motion expert, on the look-out for ways of rationalising the tasks I was given, and doing them in what seemed a more sensible fashion, though in truth I was really trying to make work easier for myself. Why stand up all day over a powerful vacuuming machine, cleaning dust from half-formed hats, when I could do the same job sitting more comfortably on a stool? The foreman quickly dispensed with that fancy idea by hiding the stool. And why not erect simple partitions to separate the various alleyways of boxes, filled with hats ready for dispatch, and which were piled high to the ceiling? When I suggested the idea to the foreman, he looked at me as if I'd landed from Mars. Later, both men perhaps saw the virtues of my suggestions when my habitual clumsiness created havoc. I totally screwed up a large vacuuming machine by allowing the progress note to be sucked in. Production was halted to allow the engineers to strip the machine and retrieve the document, which was vital for the hats' progress through the factory. I was moved to another department, where I managed to set in train a bowling-alley sequence when I stumbled and knocked over rank after rank of boxes of hats, all neatly ordered and stacked, but now sent cascading into a confused jumble at the far end of the warehouse.

Needless to say, it was very easy for a naïve schoolboy, keen to follow instructions, to be led astray by mischievous workmates, and I predictably fell victim to the timeless regime of practical jokes reserved for all newcomers. I trotted off to the engineers to ask for a left-handed screwdriver, later asking an engineer for the glass-headed hammer, returning on both occasions to applause and laughter from conspiring workmates. On my first lunch break in the hat factory, I innocently followed a workmate's directions into the managers' dining room, whence I was ejected by a besuited figure and sent back to the ranks of grinning workmates queuing for their lunch in the workers' canteen. It turned out there were three separate dining facilities (for managers, foremen and rank-and-file workers), the distinctions not dictated by the dirt of the workplace, by oily work-clothes or overalls. It was all about status and rank, and it irritated me intensely. I'd spotted yet another perfect example of the English class system at work, right under my nose at the Failsworth Hat Company. (True to form, Uncle Joe didn't dine in any of the canteens. He simply slipped round the corner to eat alone at home, part of his characteristic existence, from his motorbike to his work – alone by choice, with the exception of his visits to our house.)

Another of my jobs was working as a temporary postman before Christmas. Once, working on the post, I fell victim to the most traumatic of set-ups. I was working in the van, delivering to outlying houses and remote spots. We pulled up outside a derelict-looking farm house and the driver ordered me to deliver the mail. I approached the house up a steep flight of steps, to discover a crazy filthy old lady sitting on the top step, her face plastered with lipstick, her legs akimbo, skirt to her knees – but with no knickers. I dropped the mail and fled back to the van, where the driver was helpless with laughter at the sight of my terrified face.

Paid vacation work brought about a change in my status at home. I was now a working youth, and contributing to the household income. Local custom demanded that I hand over my unopened pay packet to my mother at the end of the week, and in return I was given the few shillings she thought appropriate.

I was keen to earn as much as I could, and had heard from a school friend about better paid jobs at a cake factory in Oldham. Though it annoyed Joe (whose loyalty to Failsworth Hat Company was a bit of a mystery), I promptly transferred my allegiance from hats to cakes. Working in the hat factory had been routine and undemanding. Cake manufacture proved utterly different. I was totally unprepared for the physical demands of the job: working in a roasting stamina-sapping and sweaty hothouse. The factory was dominated by massive ovens, some 10 yards long, through which tons of cakes trundled on metal conveyor belts. Large greasy trays, packed with tins of sloppy ingredients, were slid in at one end, travelling through the ovens for the time needed to bake that particular batch, and emerging as cakes at a steady march at the far end. The worst job, naturally enough given to newcomers, was to remove the fiery trays as they emerged from the ovens, and slot them into waiting racks. It was a very bad spot to work. First, you were assailed by the relentless heat pouring from the open ovens. Then came the unstoppable flow of hot, heavy trays. The job was much worse if you were small like me. I could only fully grasp the trays by standing on tiptoes. If you dropped a tray onto the tiled floor (and we all did) the resounding clatter was raucously applauded across the factory floor – but still the trays kept coming. You had to kick aside the fallen cakes and burning hot tray, to deal with the next oncoming batch, before they too clattered to the floor. There were breaks of course, but the blistering march of cakes seemed to go on and on: an endless flow of heat and a never-ending parade of cakes and trays. In the process, I regularly burned the inside of my lower arms (again, because of my height), and the sweltering monotony was periodically interrupted by the crash of falling trays, and the factory-wide chorus, 'It's on the floor!'.

Work was even more intense ahead of the arrival of government health inspectors. Ovens were shut down and all hands turned to the buckets, mops and cleaning chores.

Even that, rigorous enough, was as nothing compared to the cleaning frenzy that prefaced the arrival of inspectors from Marks and Spencer, to whose shops much of the produce was heading.

I tried to convince myself that I was, at least for the time being, a working man. My workmates knew differently, and I was teased mercilessly for still being at school, and therefore being a clever clogs. The first time I pulled out my *Manchester Guardian* in the canteen, my workmates laid down their own newspapers and cigarettes, gathered round me in a semicircle and mockingly applauded. Worse followed. As I held out the paper to turn over the page, someone lit one corner of the paper. Before I realised, half the *Manchester Guardian* was alight – to the incredible glee of my workmates. The arsonist grinned, leaned over and whispered in my ear, 'That'll fucking learn you!'. But within days we were all friends, united by slogging away together at the same lousy job. On my very last day, as I was leaving for Paris and thence to university, and as a sign of friendship, two of the bigger men suddenly grabbed me and dropped me into a vast hopper of cocoa powder. More applause: no matter that the dirt from my work clothes and boots would add a distinct flavour to the subsequent chocolate cakes.

One of the revelations of factory life was the existence of industrial theft, sometimes for its own sake. Some people took enormous risks merely for the hell of it, or simply to get something over the management, or to prove they could outwit security. At first I was quite shocked by what I learned. Our mother had raised us to regard theft as a mortal sin. She fairly glowed with indignation when telling cautionary tales about people who stole. Though transportation to Van Diemen's Land was no longer a legal punishment for theft, we grew up knowing that our mother would like to see the policy revived. Even so, tales about local people stealing from the workplace were rife. Some were told as funny stories (though not by our mother); others recounted disapprovingly. One of our neighbours had removed an entire truck full of wooden crates from the Ferranti factory simply to fuel our Guy Fawkes bonfire, only to discover, when they arrived, that they had stolen the wrong crates; these ones were filled with electronic parts. His greatest triumph was thus to smuggle the crates back into the factory compound without being detected. Years later, when I bought my first house from a man who worked in the railway carriage works, I discovered paint and wood which looked suspiciously like British Rail items. I was warned: 'Never whistle outside a house owned by a man from the railway carriage works: it might move off'.

Theft from the workplace, despite elaborate efforts to prevent it, was simply part of factory life. A permanent game of cat and mouse was played out between factory security and enterprising thieves. Some were merely desperate (stealing fuel for domestic fires) but others stole to order: tools, bricks, nuts and bolts. It was in the cake factory in Oldham, however, that I became fully aware of the bizarre ingenuity and extent of industrial theft. The handful of individuals involved seemed to take the factory security system as a personal challenge, and were determined to beat it at all cost. I couldn't believe that it was worth risking your job, and even prosecution, to steal a few cakes.

One of my workmates stole only the more costly cakes, designed for weddings and receptions, and then sold them. The more valuable the cake, the greater the ingenuity required, and our man was particularly adept. His favourite trick was to climb into the factory through a back window, fill a hold-all with expensive cakes, then climb back out again, before walking round to the front gate to check in the bag, filled with stolen goods, at the security gate. When he left work, he reclaimed the bag of cakes, chatting amiably with the guards as he walked off with his contraband.

Revelations of the illicit complexities of life in a factory took me far beyond the theft of cakes. The factory was a place where all forms of illicit activity took place, though it surprised me, a callow teenager, when I began to learn about it. I quickly learned for example, that the lift in one corner of the cake factory, which was designed to transfer foodstuffs between floors, was periodically off-limits and out of service, normally at lunch time. It was easy to stop the lift between floors by opening the gate, and the lift was thus a regular venue for sexual encounters. It must have been one of the North's most unattractive rendezvous for love-making. The couple had to jostle for space with trolleys packed with damaged and discarded cakes (heading for mulching and recycling into parkin), greasy racks of trays, and the lift's oily gate. Not surprisingly, when the occupants' mid-day love-making reached its height, the lift gave out a rhythmic metallic wheezing and grating: a give-away about what was happening. Everyone knew who was involved, though it took me some time to work it out. These amorous interludes were simply accepted as yet another quirky feature of factory life: some people stole cakes, others used the factory lift for sexual trysts. In my teenage innocence I was initially shocked by all this, especially by the boasting about theft. But the stories of lust in the lift merely added more evidence to the evolving mysteries of human sexuality. In any case, the creaking reality of sex in a factory lift came nowhere near the extravagant sexual escapades described by mates in Failsworth who claimed new sexual conquests most weekends. Theirs was, of course, mere boastful teenage fantasy, but it inevitably dazzled those of us who listened in confusion and ignorant admiration.

In my last three years at school, as I slipped back and forth between various jobs and school, it gradually dawned on me that I was amazingly lucky. I worked at a string of tedious jobs only because I wanted to, and I was free to use the money (at least the amount my mother handed back to me) more or less as I wished. Most of the people I worked with, however, had no such option. The men and women I saw heading to and from work early each morning, the people I worked alongside in local factories, were all there from necessity, employed in jobs they heartily disliked. In any case, how could you *enjoy* working on the steaming wet side in the hat factory, in the permanent stink of the rubber factory at the end of our street, or in the incessant clatter of a cotton mill? Where was the satisfaction in the smelly heat of a cake factory? But they all had mouths to feed and bills to pay. I was one of the lucky ones. I was working for myself, and for the next trip to France.

★ ★ ★

It was at precisely this time that the Prime Minister, Harold Macmillan, raised many people's hackles – certainly mine – by his remark that most British people had 'never had it so good'. When I looked at my fellow workmates in Failsworth and Oldham, his remarks seemed to make no sense whatsoever. Yet there *was* evidence that life was indeed getting better for more and more people. And I could see it in my own family and in the neighbourhood. The evidence was small-scale – insignificant even – but it was enough to reflect the deeper shifts that were transforming the face of Britain.

The phrase 'You've never had it so good' dominated the 1959 General Election, and has ever since stuck in the popular memory as the defining theme in that year's Tory victory. In fact Harold Macmillan first used the phrase, in a more innocent and more specific comment, at a Conservative rally in July 1957, but it proved to be both a populist cliché and a clever observation about the changing face of Britain. It also served to persuade many people that they were indeed better off under the Conservatives. It was easy enough for politicians to point to the undeniable and obvious signs of material improvements in the country at large. Moreover, Macmillan's comment seemed to converge with a more intellectual analysis, notably John Kenneth Galbraith's 1958 *The Affluent Society*, though admittedly he was writing about post-war USA, that the West had entered an entirely new and unprecedented phase of widespread material wellbeing. Nevertheless, during the election campaign I railed against Harold Macmillan's slogan. Coming from an Old Etonian, blessed at birth with the proverbial silver spoon, it sounded more like a sneering insult than an undeniable truth. But Macmillan had clearly spotted an indisputable fact: British people had begun to own items, and to enjoy forms of leisure, which they had merely dreamed about only a few years earlier. Our family, untypical in many ways, and bobbing along towards the bottom of the social pile, also began to see improvements. We now had a little more money, and hire purchase allowed us to acquire some of the appliances that were transforming domestic life everywhere.

Up to 1957 our mother managed a precarious financial juggling act, though without our grandparent's help we would have sunk. One Christmas Eve, Grandpa marched me to a butcher's shop in Oldham, collected a chicken, then dispatched me home on the bus, clutching what I realised was Christmas lunch. That simple act was typical of the years before and immediately after Dad's death, when our grandparents provided incalculable help and support. Clothes, shoes, holidays, food and treats, all and more were simply part of who and what our grandparents were.

Our mother made regular use of hire purchase (known as HP), by which you paid for goods in instalments, not actually owning them until the last payment was made. Buying things 'on tick' had been a way of life, even though it had obvious problems of its own, and was often criticised in the press. But for us – and millions more – HP offered a short cut to better times. When we were small, Mum often bought our clothes from a catalogue and paid off the bill in small instalments. Sometimes even my shoes came through the post, with the predictable results. Shoes which claimed to be my size turned out to be a painful exercise in Chinese foot-binding: too small, too tight, pinching, rough at the heel and almost always quickly worn through. I managed eventually to break down their resistance by simply pounding the streets in them, moulding the shoes to my own particular shape and needs, but it all came at the cost of blisters, pinched toes and sore feet. There were times too when Mum even hired items of clothing for special occasions. The smart jackets and coats in which Alan and I appeared for Whitsuntide and holidays mysteriously disappeared shortly afterwards: they had been returned to the outfitters.

From 1957 onwards, things began to improve. My own summer earnings augmented the family income, at least for a short period. Mum began to earn more money, largely through her spare-time ladies' hairdressing in the kitchen. The initial spare cash went on home improvements, some barely noticeable at first: fresh rolls of linoleum in the kitchen and bedroom for instance. Pride of place, however, went to the new 'tiled fireplace' which replaced an old black-leaded open grate and fire. We also succumbed to the fashionable craze for having flush doors, with sheets of plywood nailed on to cover the door's original features. But by far the most important and striking change in the late 1950s was the arrival of new domestic appliances. A new radio (the family's main source of information and entertainment throughout most of our childhood) was followed by a record player, bought from the Co-Op store down the road at Newton Heath. With that plugged in, I began to buy my own records, gradually filling my head with the songs from the Great American Songbook. But the real transformation was brought about by new labour-saving devices, all bought on HP. First a new vacuum cleaner, then, most important of all, a washing machine. Our mother's life was made instantly and immeasurably easier.

The stretched finances which had been a way of life as long as I could remember began to ease a little. Items once considered luxuries came within our reach, thanks largely to HP. Whenever conversation turned to HP (we discussed it at school and it regularly cropped up in the press) it provoked a sniffy distrust. I regularly met people who dismissed the very idea of HP, explaining that those who used it were throwing their money away. Better by far to *save* in order to buy household items. These arguments generally came wrapped in that distinctively English dislike of popular change. Yet for millions of people of limited means, HP was the *only* way of gaining immediate access to the goods that made life much easier. Saving up meant waiting – and that meant years of the same hard domestic labour. For people who worked long hours, often at hard or tedious jobs, the new labour-saving devices were a boon. Both the vacuum cleaner and a new simple washing machine made women's lives easier at a stroke. In our own case (in common with armies of other people) they heralded an end to age-old labour-intensive routines. Sweeping the house had previously involved a laborious sweep through the house with brush and a broom, the carpets and rugs taken outside and given a good whacking against an outside wall, or hung from a line and bashed with a cane carpet beater. Now they all succumbed to the noisy hum of a vacuum cleaner.

The most fundamental change of all was the purchase of a washing machine, and we greeted its arrival as if it had landed from outer space. (If anyone needs to be persuaded about its impact, they need only go to a poor country today to watch women bent double, labouring over their laundry at riversides, pools and plastic bowls at the kerbside.) Family washday had traditionally been the harshest and most inescapable of domestic chores, especially with a gang of grubby boys, their dirty clothes and bed-wetting problems. Washing by hand involved a back-breaking regime of soaking, boiling, washing, pummelling, rinsing and drying. Each stage was hard, and each undertaken with implements which, today, you can only find in museums or antique shops – an old boiler, a washing tub, a ribbed scrubbing board (which Alan used as a percussion instrument between washes), a posser (a tool for mixing the washing) and a mangle. Finally the damp items were hoisted to dangle above our heads from the kitchen rack.

As children, we were recruited to help with the weekly wash, which, like everything else in the house, took place in the kitchen. I was in charge of the copper-headed posser, vigorously lifting it in and out, trying to make the pile of dirty laundry swirl around in the soapy water, and generally bashing it into some kind of clean submission. I remember washday as fun. For our mother, it was very hard work: perhaps the most demanding, inescapable and unrelenting of domestic chores. Even with the dubious help of small boys, all this had to be done after a hard week's work. It was a reminder that for working-class women, home was not so much an escape from the rigours of the working week, but a mere change of location of their labouring chores. Domestic work waited for them when they got home from their paid work.

A washing machine came, then, as a blessed relief and, not surprisingly, was acquired as soon as possible, thanks to HP. It would have been pointless telling our mother that she would be better off financially to wait until she had saved enough to buy a machine outright: she needed relief sooner rather than later. And so – out with the old scrubbing board, posser and tub. We bought a Hotpoint washing machine; it was simple, clunky and noisy, but it eased Mum's life enormously. Three cheers for HP, all financial disadvantages greatly outweighed by the immediate personal and social benefits. Life became less onerous – and therefore better.

Despite the great benefits of the washing machine, the most obvious and most talked-about domestic transformation of these years was of course the arrival of the television. In our case, that had to wait till 1960, just before I left home and when Alan started work. The first set came from a relative who worked for a TV manufacturer and who could buy a set at a discount. Before then, our access to TV for special moments and big occasions (such as the 1958 World Cup from Sweden) had come largely by knocking on neighbours doors and asking if we could watch their TV. I felt uncomfortable asking, but the lure of the programmes invariably overcame my shyness.

★ ★ ★

So Harold McMillan had got it right after all. Life *had* indeed changed for the better by the late 1950s. I noticed it even in my own personal social life, as the cash-strapped existence up to my mid-teens imperceptibly gave way to much less straitened times. From 1957 onwards I had a little money in my pocket, largely because I was able to work early mornings and in vacations. From 1957 I had enough money to cover all the things I enjoyed doing outside of school: travel, football, books, records. All this – small amounts in themselves – required a spending power that we simply did not have only a few years earlier.

Until the late 1950s eating out had been a rare treat. Our grandparents had taken us for meals (normally fish and chips) in Oldham, but we really only ate out at weddings, funerals and on our seaside holidays. Meals at the seaside boarding house took place like military drill: precisely timed and with no room for manoeuvre. At set times we dutifully returned to our Blackpool boarding house to be summoned to the table by the landlady's gong in the hall, to sit at our assigned table, and to be served whatever the landlady decided we wanted that day. The arrangement of cutlery confused me: which implements were needed for this dish or that? Brusque as ever, grandpa had no such doubts, simply dispensing with all of them. Because of his damaged hand, he used a single spoon for everything, shovelling food round his plate, pressing it against a slice of bread, before wolfing it, and then telling the assembled dining room how much he'd enjoyed it. But such moments of dining out were rare. Then, in my late teens, suddenly dining out emerged as one of life's new pleasures.

The social life of a 17–18 year old, in and around central Manchester, demanded a few shillings in one's pocket. On breaks from work in the Manchester Central Library, for example, we headed to the new coffee bars in the centre of town. We could linger over a single cup of frothy coffee for as long as we liked. Real coffee came with what seemed a genuine 'continental' ambiance. They reminded me of France, though they quickly established themselves as distinctive features of British city life. The new 'tea centres' were much the same but, oddly enough, because they served the national drink they seemed much less exotic, even though the waitresses were dark-skinned and wore saris. Lingering in a coffee bar along with my school mates was a sign of our growing sophistication. At much the same time, we also discovered the first Indian restaurants. We now know that they were not, strictly speaking, Indian, as most of the owners originated from Pakistan. Nor were most of the cheap dishes on offer recognisable to most Indians. But they utterly transformed our lives. Along with a couple of school mates I scoured central Manchester for bargains: Indian restaurants offering low price 'specials'. So there we were, dining in a restaurant, enjoying the luxury of a more-or-less clean tablecloth, lolling around after a meal. Though I would always be fantasising about being back at a Parisian café, it was still enjoyable to be undisturbed by the clatter of meals in the kitchen at home – not having to clear up, wash up, and clear off to make way for the first shampoo and set of the evening. France had already introduced me to the custom of eating out, though always choosing the cheapest items in the cheapest of places. Counting the thousands of francs in my pocket beforehand to make sure I could afford it, then lingering over the cheapest dish, became a simple pleasure. A *croque monsieur* in a Parisian side street, or the cheapest curry in a basement Manchester curry house – they now look pretty meagre, but it didn't feel that way at the time. They were, of course, signs of better times.

I suppose, too, all this was the beginning of adult life. Most of my school mates had left school at 15 for full-time work, and the handful of us left behind, though treated as young adults by our sensible headmaster, were still trapped in our school blazers. This felt ever more irksome as we emerged into early manhood. A stubbly chin and a school blazer didn't quite go together. We acted and talked like young men, and increasingly felt ourselves to be men, not schoolboys. Yet even as we lounged around in a basement Indian restaurant, pretending to be sophisticated lounge lizards, our blazers gave us away. For all the stubble, for all the bravado about France and all things French, we were just schoolboys.

Some of my school friends seemed to have plenty of cash in their pockets in those last two years at school, but even those of us from poorer homes now had enough to enjoy some of the relatively simple pleasures of Manchester in the late 1950s. We were all united in one great ambition. All of us who stayed at school until 18 were itching to break away: to secure the necessary qualifications from school before escaping to work or into higher education. We all needed to get away.

CHAPTER 13

All Change

Joe Eyre had been a frequent visitor both before and after our father's death. In my teens, he had provided me with a homely retreat where I could study, away from the clatter of life in our crowded kitchen. In fact Joe was as much a feature of my family life as any other person. Of course we did not appreciate, in our early years, the human and emotional entanglements that lay behind Joe's presence. We now know that the love affair between our mother and Joe had begun before our father's death, and it continued for years. I was as close to all this as anyone, but to this day I can't be sure how long the affair had been going on. At first, of course, I was a child, innocent of what was happening and unaware of the human complexities around me. I was happy simply to see Uncle Joe on his visits to our father. By my mid-teens (and notwithstanding my own haziness about sexual matters) it slowly dawned on me that something was 'going on' between Joe and my mother, though I cannot tell, even now, *when* I knew precisely. The reality dawned slowly, over a long period. I suppose too my awareness of the affair was itself a reflection of my own growing up. I began to pick up particular moments, incidents and gestures between the two of them: those tell-tale, give-away signals – almost insignificant in themselves but revealing when seen close up.

The evidence, however, was there for all to see. Throughout the 1950s Joe was the *only* man who visited, alone, on a regular basis. He often brought flowers for Mum. He took Ian on holiday, and there were plenty of photographs of Ian as a child in Joe's company. But there was more to all this than the accumulation of hard factual evidence. A string of intangibles – particularly the way other people responded – became revealing indications. As I grew older, I was struck by how quickly the atmosphere changed when people mentioned Joe's name in my presence. It was as if they preferred *not* to talk about him, or were happier to move on to another subject. A strange reluctance entered people's conversation whenever Joe's name cropped up. People who never hesitated to give you trenchant opinions about Mr X and Mrs Y became oddly circumspect when it came to Joe Eyre. My grandmother babbled with endless gossip about the world at large, and about human shortcomings, and she should know – having apparently left a trail of broken hearts around Oldham. (To this day I find it hard to believe the family legend about her and the coalman.) But even dear old Grandma was struck oddly dumb on the topic of Joe Eyre. Until that is, she advanced into her talkative and revealing old age. I gradually realised that the silences, the hesitations and the change of direction in conversation were as revealing as the more tangible evidence.

It was as if there was an embargo on talking about Joe, at least in front of the children, in case an indiscreet remark might leave the wrong (that is, the correct) impression. Yet all the adults in the family, and lots of people in the neighbourhood, were clearly aware of the relationship. It must have been obvious at work (for years the two of them worked in the same factory). And it was surely evident to neighbours who saw Joe crossing the road regularly to arrive at our front door clutching a bunch of flowers. Most telling of all, it was startlingly obvious in the person of my brother Ian.

Ian was 10 years younger than me, eight years younger than Alan. He was still at nursery when I was 15 and was only seven when I left home. From the first he looked nothing like his two brothers. Alan and I were, and remain, obvious brothers: similar features, build and similar small stocky frame. We were, and remain, brotherly in a variety of ways, despite our very different careers and lives. Ian, however, is distinct in every physical respect. No one, looking at the three of us together, would imagine him to be our brother. As he himself confessed, he looks like a stranger who has accidentally strolled into a family photograph. But glance at the photos of Joe and Ian together and the reality dawns. Joe and Ian: father and son.

Not surprisingly, we simply thought of ourselves as three brothers, sons of the same father. As long as we all lived in the house together as a family, the question of Ian's paternity was never raised. For a start I didn't really think about it until well into my teens. Even then, I would not have dared raise it. We simply accepted that Ian was our younger brother.

Through all this, and even now, half a century later, Joe remains an enigma. He floated in and out of our lives, often part of the family, but he was also simply a neighbour from across the street. Joe was a kind man, apparently happy in his unobtrusive lifestyle, content to drift quietly through life, only assertive at work when faced by a colleague's failings, and angered, socially, only by my own rare teenage misdemeanours. Joe was not a man who gave or showed affection easily. Rarely demonstrative, he was generally happier to let his feelings reveal themselves in small gestures. I now realise that he loved Ian, though he was always considerate to me (Alan's life led him in a different directions). I assume too that he loved our mother. But did she love him? Once again, I hesitate and feel a sense of inappropriate intrusion.

They had Ian in common and that alone may have been enough to bring Joe to our home regularly, but they never went anywhere together in public. Though there were occasional family teas and celebrations when Joe put in an appearance, they did not 'walk out' together as a couple. In fact, through all the years I knew Joe, he had very little public social life. In the years when British life was brightening up, when people found themselves with a little more cash and now able to enjoy themselves more, Joe remained wedded to his simple and isolated existence. His old pleasures also began to fade. His pride and joy, the Rudge motorbike, stood unused from one month to another. He occasionally wheeled it out into the back yard for a thorough clean and mechanical tinkering, but by the late 1950s his motor-cycling days were over. Joe was aging, slowing down, coughing more (not surprising given his endless smoking). It was evident too that the years of Japanese brutality were catching up on him. I don't remember his condition in 1945, but the photographs he showed me, taken by the Americans on his release, revealed one of those appalling images, so commonplace in 1945. It was the face of millions of people across Europe and Asia, released from camps and prisons and emerging from the war's destruction, staring blankly at the camera. Joe's photos in 1945 were of a wreck of a man, teetering on the edge, skeletal, vacant-eyed, totally blank and confused. Although he had obviously fleshed out and stabilised over the following decade, he remained a slight, sinewy figure, haunted by the terrible things he had endured and witnessed between 1942 and 1945.

Looking back to all this, and trying to make sense of it, I worry that perhaps I'm imagining too much, reconstructing too complex and elaborate a narrative for the period when Joe first began to talk about the war in the months immediately after I came home from my first visit to France in 1956. Perhaps too I tend to see Joe's experiences reflected through my own personal awakening to a wider world. There is, however, no denying the coincidence of timing. Late in 1956, Joe began to talk about the war, about the camps, and about the Japanese. True, this was also the period when I began to spend more time in his house to study. Before and after I'd finished my homework or reading, as I innocently grilled him about the war, he began to open up, though initially dismissing my new-found curiosity with a smoky wave of his cigarette. Joe simply did not accept my enthusiasm for France. He just wouldn't have it: he refused to accept that France was remotely worth talking about, despite never having been there. France was abroad and abroad was beastly. There was nowhere, *nowhere*, like home – like England. He had, it is true, circled the globe – South Africa, Malaya, Formosa, Japan, Manila, and finally the USA, before sailing home on the *Queen Mary*. But every leg of that three-year journey had been as a soldier or as a prisoner. Joe had seen the world, and he clearly thought that it left a great deal to be desired.

The only compliments he paid to foreigners were reserved for the USA. The Americans had, after all, saved him, rescued him from what he and all his fellow prisoners believed was certain death. The prisoners often talked about what they would do in the face of a Japanese defeat and their captors' threat to execute all prisoners. (To a man they all gave thanks for the atomic bomb when they heard about it.) The Americans had saved him, then restored him to a modicum of health, and treated him grandly en route across the Pacific and thence across the USA.

Even so, Joe shared the traditional Englishman's reservations about Americans (the 'Yanks' in his parlance). They were brash, noisy and vulgar. When he looked at foreigners in general, Joe clearly thought that Americans were the best of a bad lot. All this, never expressed vehemently, was in keeping with attitudes to the world at large that prevailed throughout the neighbourhood, although Joe could at least claim that his views were based on his experience of having travelled the world in khaki. And who was I, aged 14 and upwards, to challenge him on the basis of a few weeks in France? I suppose too, in all these conversations with Joe, I was beginning to develop my own intellectual curiosity about big issues (though on the basis of very little knowledge) and was using Joe as a sounding board for fledgling ideas. Joe's reaction was to fall back on traditional deep-seated English jingoism, but all mixed and shaken with his own wartime experiences.

All this evolved slowly, over many evening and weekend visits to his house. As we fenced around each other, and as Joe began to talk about the war, he added new bits of information for me to absorb and deal with. The end result was that I learned more perhaps about Joe's war than anyone else. He certainly had not had time to tell his late wife. Perhaps he had told his mother; perhaps my mother too? Much later, I realised that I had been a very privileged audience, and in the process I grew ever closer to Joe, though there remained unbridgeable barriers between us. We were a generation apart – and divided by much more than years – and we lived in a society which maintained clear divides between generations. Convention and politeness demanded a distance. Still, we became friends, as far as that was possible between a youth and a middle-aged man. More important perhaps, I gained Joe's confidence and he entrusted me with some of his most deep-seated secrets. There were however two issues we did *not* discuss: his late wife and his relationship with my mother.

Then, quite suddenly and unexpectedly, the question of Joe and Mum became an urgent issue, and I was openly drawn into their relationship, piggy in the middle in a most painful and anxious period. I became a reluctant eavesdropper to their private lives.

★ ★ ★

Getting into university had become a pressing concern in my last year at school and I spent more and more time studying in Joe's house. Working at home was impossible because of the knots of women lining the kitchen-cum-hair-dressing salon, and the endless chatter between Mum and her customers. Just when I needed space and silence, I could get neither. I couldn't complain though, because our mother had finally found a way of making enough money to handle the house and family adequately. In any case, I'd also come to enjoy and value my time with Joe.

Although I spent most of my time in Joe's house studying, I inevitably spent a lot of time relaxing in his company. He was a perfect host, never intruding or interrupting when I was working (except to ask if I needed yet another cup of tea), but always available for a chat. I became an audience of one in Joe's reminiscences about the war. But in 1960 I became much more than a visiting schoolboy. Quite suddenly I became the mediator between Joe and my mother. Until then, she had rarely come up in conversation. Joe didn't need to ask about her. After all, she was just across the street, and Joe had never been reluctant about visiting. Then, out of the blue, something went wrong between the two of them. At least it went wrong for Joe.

In the early summer of 1960 my mind was focused on my work, and Alan was leaving school and heading for his apprenticeship, when an old friend of our mother's from pre-war days presented himself. Alan McDonald and his wife had been friends with our parents, the two couples often going to dances together in the late 1930s. Recently widowed, he was obviously keen to renew his friendship with Mum. She was still youngish, lively and energetic. She was also, I think, anxious to find some way out of the grind that had been her daily life for the best part of 20 years. Although she was now a little better off, she remained burdened by three sons and a regime of hard work. It was not too difficult to see how her head might be turned by the prospects of a better new life.

Alan McDonald began to show an interest in her, and she was obviously attracted. For the first time, to my knowledge, she began to go out on dates. I was completely confused by the turn of events. For a start, wasn't it supposed to be the other way round? Weren't mothers supposed to be the ones concerned about their children's emergent love lives? Once again, I found myself in an older person's shoes, worrying about what my mother was up to. I wanted to see her happily settled with someone who could give her the comfort she had been denied. But what was wrong with Joe Eyre?

The new rival was utterly different from Joe in every respect. He dressed in quite an eye-catching style, and often wore a flower in his button-hole, rounding off the image by sporting a pencil-thin moustache. He liked to say he looked like Douglas Fairbanks Jnr. He was affable and easy-going, had a general air of bravado, and was always ready with a quip or a joke. His sharp-witted mordant sense of humour appealed to me. (Years later, leaving a family funeral in Oldham Crematorium on a biting winter's day, he announced to the assembled relatives as we all squeezed into an enormous Austin Princess: 'There's one thing to be said for the deceased. He'll be warmer than the rest of us.')

I wasn't surprised to learn that he had been a band leader before the war, and I enjoyed listening to him on the piano, rattling out inter-war tunes, and even old music hall songs from before 1914. His was an image and style perfectly suited to running a pub on the other side of town. He was a natural 'mine host': the amiable chap behind the bar, ready to swap yarns and jokes throughout the evening as customers downed their beer. There was, however, another side to him which I remained ignorant of until much later. For the time being, all I knew was that he was keen on our mother, and she seemed happy in his company. And as her children, we were simply dragged along in the emotional undertow of their new friendship. Joe, on the other hand, seemed utterly lost.

The sudden appearance of a rival was clearly a severe blow for Joe. He did two things. He backed away from her, and then turned to me – a fixture in his front room and all of 18 – as a go-between. Although I had tried to steer clear of their relationship, I was now drawn in. Joe was a proud man, shy too, and faced by a rival and by Mum's obvious interest in the newcomer, Joe simply withdrew. I was secretly astonished that he didn't put up more resistance, more of a fight. I should have known that wasn't his way. After all, hadn't he told me many times how the camps had taught him to be cautious, even to turn the other cheek? Though the war was receding fast, Joe's memories of those events remained undimmed and lurked just below the surface. The golden rule was: best not to say anything. Let matters take their course. There was a time when it was essential to remain silent and let events take their course. He told me of men who hadn't, and who had not survived. It was a brutal lesson learned the hard way and had been basic to survival in a Japanese camp, but I thought it made no sense in 1960.

It wasn't, then, in Joe's temperament or experience to be confrontational. Instead, in the summer of 1960, he retreated, mentally and physically. He simply stayed at home. All direct contact between Joe and Mum ceased. But he had on hand someone who might be a useful messenger, a go-between – me.

Perhaps Joe had spoken to her, and perhaps I was the last desperate throw of his emotional dice? I now became Joe's envoy, shuttling across the street, formally to study, returning informally as the bearer of cryptic messages. I found my new role as emissary immensely troubling. It was hard enough coping with my own 18-year-old love pangs (a clever girlfriend who had already gone off to Cambridge leaving me behind, worrying in my school blazer) without becoming embroiled in the entanglement of three adults – one of them my mother. As usual, Joe didn't say much, preferring to give me simple supplications to take across the street. On successive trips I relayed a string of enigmatic verbal messages:

' Tell your mother not to do anything hasty.'

'Tell her she knows how I feel about her.'

'Tell her she knows my situation.'

I was unsure that I should even be involved, and I conveyed the messages clumsily and painfully. My mother received my hesitant messages impassively. She gave nothing away. I don't recall her saying anything in reply to Joe's entreaties. Perhaps, like me, she too was embarrassed. Which mother would welcome her young son carrying communications from the lover she had decided to ditch? Not a single message went the other way. She had clearly made up her mind.

She talked a little about her new beau, telling me how long they'd known each other and how he was a relatively prosperous man. She seemed unduly impressed by the fact that he used an accountant. I tentatively suggested that didn't mean very much. A pub's finances were a little more complex than earning a weekly wage, but that didn't necessarily indicate prosperity. I hated these conversations, and felt I was treading a delicate line. I didn't want to give the impression that I had doubts about her new friend, even though I *did* have doubts about the speed of events. (My instinctive caution was well established even at 18.) There was, too, a selfish element about all this. I was keen to leave in a few weeks' time, safe in the knowledge that she was in good hands. Yet everything was happening so quickly, so unexpectedly, that it left me uneasy.

For a start, I hardly knew her new beau. Although he was not unfriendly to me or Alan, it was clear enough that he had no idea how to deal with children and young adults. He had no children of his own, and the three boys who were part of his new liaison must have seemed both a burden and a challenge. Though he was obviously attracted to our mother, her sons – all part of the deal – clearly did not figure in his calculations. At first, I thought it was to his great credit that he was willing to involve himself with a woman with three children. Lots of men would simply baulk at the prospect, and find a gaggle of stepsons one burden too many. Later, I realised that he had not thought through the complexities and problems of inheriting three sons. The reality of having us in his life dawned on him later, long after the marriage. In the event, he was spared the full impact of a houseful of boys. I promptly left for university and Alan started work. That left Ian, seven years old, the only child at home.

Ian posed a problem for the new man. He was a living reminder, under the same roof, of his love rival Joe Eyre. Ian looked like Joe even then and must have raised troubling thoughts for the new man in our mother's life. In the event, and running ahead of the story, the relationship between Ian, both as a child and a teenager, and the new man in the house was to be deeply unhappy, and not resolved until Ian left home at the age of 15. In many respects it was easiest for me. The upsetting role of go-between simply fizzled out, and in any case I knew that once I took the bus south my life would soon take me in a very different direction.

Through this entire domestic saga, which had unfolded rapidly over the summer, I worried about Joe. One of his messages had really perplexed me: 'Tell her, she knows my situation'. To my naïve mind, his situation seemed simple. He was a widower who had paid court to our mother for years, and who had a son by her, though that was not recognised publically. Why did Joe not make the obvious move? Why didn't he ask her to marry him?

I was middle aged before I felt able to ask my aging mother the obvious question: 'Why didn't you marry Joe?' 'He never asked,' she said. That left unanswered the obvious question: why didn't he ask? Everything suggests that Joe loved her, and thought of her as his woman or partner – whatever the appropriate word might be. Marrying would have made sense, and would have been widely welcomed. I am sure our mother would have accepted. But in the summer of 1960 Joe lost his chance.

His 'situation' was not as simple as I imagined when I was 18, and in time I came to accept that there was little about Joe that was as simple, as straightforward, or as obvious as it ought to have been. His mother lived on, and as long as she survived he could not commit himself to anyone else, not even to the mother of his only child, the widow of his best friend across the street. At first glance, this determination to care for an old lady at the cost of his own happiness seems pig-headed and odd. What was to stop Joe remarrying *and* caring for his mother? Millions of people manage to do both: have a family life of their own while caring, in one way or another, for aging parents. Why did it have to be one or the other? The only explanation that made any sense to me took me back, once again, to the scars of 1945. Joe was unflinching in his resolve to stick by his mother, the only person who had believed he had survived.

★ ★ ★

It had all happened in such a rush. Within a matter of weeks we had been told that our mother had a new beau, that they were happy together, and then that they were planning to marry. I wasn't the only one to feel confused. Quite apart from my affection for Joe, I was genuinely troubled by the speed of events. It all seemed so hasty. When I tentatively talked to Mum about the marriage, she offered vague generalities in its favour. Although I was not a starry-eyed romantic, I remained unsure whether this amounted to ideal ingredients for a marriage. But what did I know at 18? And who was I even to ask? I felt it was presumptuous even to question her.

At the same time, I was keen to see her settled before I left home. I was not worried about my brothers. I knew

Alan would be fine: he was already older than his years, much more worldly wise than me, and more than capable of looking after himself. Ian was still a small child and I simply and naïvely assumed that the new man in Mum's life would care for him. That left the problem of Joe.

But whose problem was he? What had that to do with us now? Mother had washed her hands of him, but I retained an emotional loyalty to him. I was the young friend he had adopted and helped. Despite my youth, I had been drawn into some of Joe's deepest and most private thoughts and memories. After a fashion, I had been the means for him to come to terms with his long-suppressed demons. First I had been an audience to his wartime stories, and then acted as his courier when his love affair broke down. But what could I do now, when faced by my mother's change of heart? I felt loyalty to Joe, and it distressed me to see him hurt, but I inevitably had to side with my mother. She had made up her mind, and Joe was left behind by a swirl of events which transformed family life completely – and all in a matter of weeks.

★ ★ ★

The wedding was a small gathering in the Oldham Parish Church. Mum insisted that I give her away, though my conventional response was that her father should do it. 'I want you to do it.' So once again, I found myself cast in the role of an older person. Recently a teenage confessor to a damaged POW and the go-between in a collapsing love affair, I now found myself giving away my mother as a bride. I often felt that I'd had old age thrust upon me.

The register-signing ceremony completed, the newlyweds set off to walk back down the aisle as man and wife. They'd taken only a few strides when Grandpa Wood (who had risen to the occasion, discarding his cloth cap for his ceremonial bowler) nimbly stepped from his front pew, blocked the couple's path and kissed his daughter.

This might not seem unusual or surprising – but it was. It was the first time I had seen Grandpa kiss *anyone*. It was if his tough old hide had finally cracked. A man not given to open displays of his inner feelings, he had finally kissed someone – *and in public*: a memorable family first. This refusal to show his affectionate feelings in public was not an act; not a conscious performance. It was part personal, part generational. There were certain things men simply didn't do. After my first French trip, I told him enthusiastically how Frenchmen *often* kissed in public. They even kissed *other men* in public. I should have known better. It merely confirmed his ideas about the French, and he had snorted at the very idea: enough said. Yet his flinty public behaviour was totally deceptive, and shielded the humane and affectionate man within.

Having kissed his daughter, Grandpa then vigorously shook the bridegroom's hand. The new husband was clearly pleased with Grandpa's gesture of halting the bridal procession in the aisle to be the first to congratulate the couple. But that handshake must have hurt. Grandpa used the hand devoid of all sensation (that factory accident again); receiving a hand shake from it was like trapping your hand in a closing door.

After the ceremony, we adjourned to a simple reception in the pub that would henceforth be our new home. Though the newlyweds seemed happy enough, the happiest folk by far that day were our slightly dishevelled looking grandparents. As they entered their seventies, they had at last seen their daughter rescued from the hardship that had been her lot since 1942. As was her way, Grandma smiled throughout. But she always did. She seemed to float through most days with a smile on her face, except when afflicted by one of her 'turns' (for which she regularly took a local remedy called Cecil Wood's powders). Grandma wanted people to think of her as a happy woman, even when she had little to be happy about. She presided over a dirty household, delivered terrible meals to the table, ignored all rules of domestic cleanliness and hygiene, but beamed throughout. This time however, she had plenty to beam about.

Grandpa, always happiest when filling his belly, was in his element. A lifetime of Grandma's cooking meant that the simplest of meals must have looked like *haute cuisine*. As usual he shared his pleasure with anyone close to hand, telling the assembled wedding party how much he had enjoyed his mound of sausage rolls, sandwiches and pickles. (He had said precisely the same thing, seven years earlier, on the other side of Oldham Road at the reception following Dad's funeral.) Food put him in a good mood. A hearty breakfast after one of our dawn walks on holiday, a lunch plate wiped clean by a final slice of bread each Sunday, a plentiful serving after funerals and weddings – everything was devoured, and his pleasure was always too much to keep secret. He enjoyed his food, and enjoyed telling people how much he had enjoyed it. This time, however, he took much greater pleasure from seeing his daughter remarried. Later that day, our grandparents shuffled back to Oldham. It was almost the last time I saw him. Only weeks later he was dead. He had worked in the mill until he was 70 but then, only months after retirement, he suddenly died, killed (the post-mortem revealed) by the atmospheric cotton he had inhaled for more than 50 years.

★ ★ ★

There was, of course, one man who was far from happy about all this, but he wasn't at the wedding. Joe Eyre was at home, across the street from the house we were busy vacating. As we moved home, gradually decanting into the pub, Joe effectively disappeared. Though we had moved only a short distance, it was far enough away to lose sight of him. Joe had walked past our front door every single day. On many days he'd been a visitor. All that had stopped when it was clear that Mum had made up her mind to remarry. Joe simply retreated into his house, into his favourite chair, close to the fire, where he smoked and gazed into the fireplace for hours. Through all the years I'd known him, from childhood to early manhood, he had occupied the same spot, the same chair, when we talked together, and he remained sitting there when I disappeared into the front room to study. Now he had been abandoned, stranded in the house with his bedridden blind mother. This devotion to his mother's care, and his refusal to countenance any other binding commitment as long as she lived had destroyed whatever chances he may have had of married happiness. Perhaps he'd gone beyond being able to commit himself to another woman? All this now seems mere historical guess work, but even after a lifetime devoted to historical guess work I remain perplexed by Joe's behaviour. I think that he wanted to marry but held back because of what he described as 'my situation', only to find himself trumped, unexpectedly, by a rival. Mum wanted to be married – to the right man. For years, Joe had been the right man. But in the summer of 1960 he found himself gazumped.

What was left for him now? His job? Caring for a frail and fading old lady? (She died shortly afterwards.) He had a son, of course, my brother Ian, but he too had gone, removed from easy access and now formally in the care of

Mum's new husband, who was a total stranger to the child, as he was to the rest of us. Everyone accepted the polite fiction that Ian was our father's third son. In September 1960, Joe thus suffered a double loss. The woman he had loved for years had cut him adrift, and his son was absorbed into another man's family. The stark truth remained: Joe was now marooned and on his own. I was to learn, many years later, that so too was Ian.

★ ★ ★

The wedding ended, the couple went on their honeymoon and my brothers and I slowly transferred to the pub. The idea of living in a pub did not appeal to me in the least. True, I was busy packing and getting ready to leave – but not for the pub. I was heading elsewhere, and I never came to think of the new place as home. I had the very odd feeling in September 1960, not so much that I'd left home, but that home had simply collapsed around me. I was oddly homeless.

CHAPTER 14

Breaking Away

By the time I took the bus south to the Potteries, the British Road Services truck had already carted away a battered trunk containing all the things I needed as student. A few hours later I was bedded down in my new campus home. Part stately home, part army camp, the University College of North Staffordshire (later Keele University) presented a strange architectural image. It looked, said another new arrival, like a cross between Butlins and Belsen. We were housed in ex-army Nissen huts and some of my contemporaries complained about them, but I couldn't understand their objections. They were centrally heated, had indoor lavatories and bathrooms, and meals were provided a short walk away. It was the most comfortable place I'd ever lived in. What more did you need?

My first evening as an undergraduate was not, however, what I expected. Our 'Warden' (which sounded to me too much like an officer in Strangeways) invited us to a sherry party. I had never drunk sherry before.

'Sweet or dry, Mr Walvin?'

I hadn't a clue (how could a drink be dry?). So I said 'Sweet'. Uncertain how to drink from what looked like a glass thimble, I took what seemed the obvious route and slugged it back in two simple quaffs.

'Another one, Mr Walvin?'

'Yes please.'

The man serving the drinks was very generous with the sherry. But he looked odd: his face had been burned as a wartime pilot. After about four refills in 20 minutes, I was distinctly squiffy. At which point we were joined by the man's small terrier. The dog had a sanitary towel strapped round her rear end. Two dozen pairs of 18-year-old eyes stared in disbelief at the wretched animal. Our host explained: 'She's in season'.

'Ah! I see. That makes perfect sense!'

I was totally confused by the entire scene. All this – a savage war wound, too much sherry and a dog sporting a sanitary towel, only hours after I'd left Failsworth, felt as if I'd walked onto the set of the Goon Show. Thus passed my first and unforgettably surreal evening at university. Fortunately I hitched up with another new arrival (who seemed more at ease with the sherry routines) and who became a lifelong friend, and we stumbled out to dinner. There the opening item was a loyal toast to the Queen – another first.

I woozily went to bed, the overhead spars of the Nissen hut gently swaying side to side, and I seriously worried whether I'd made the right move.

★ ★ ★

Had I been a year older I would have experienced Nissen huts in their more basic reality – as a National Service soldier. We'd avoided that by a matter of months, and made the simple switch from schoolboys to students. We'd missed the worst of everything – no wars or soldiering for us – and we now received the best of everything. We entered four years of easy-going studying, without having to pay a penny. It was, without doubt, a very cushy billet.

We formed a small select bunch (only a tiny percentage of our age group went on to higher education) and were about to enjoy the best the state could provide – and all for free. Better still, I was actually *paid* to study. I suddenly found myself rewarded for having been a swot by being given more money than I'd ever dreamed of. With the cheque from my State Scholarship I opened my first bank account and promptly bought my first overcoat. Money which had, only weeks earlier, been accumulated by months of early morning paper rounds round Failsworth, now simply rolled into my new National Provincial account, courtesy of the British tax-payer. I was astonished by the generosity of the system. Almost up to the last moment, I hadn't given a thought to the student grant, and it had never occurred to me that being a student would mean being well off. It was very welcome of course, but it also seemed unfair, and at first I felt guilty and had to justify (to myself at least) my comfortable existence at other people's expense. My former workmates were still slogging away in their factories, and not earning much more for a week's hard work than I was given for merely sitting in a library and listening to lectures. My brother, now an apprentice, was working each week for less. It was as if I'd won some kind of lottery, and it was all the more surprising because it was totally unexpected. As I hunkered down to the luxury of being a student, the only real decision I had to make was what exactly I wanted to study. At that time Keele was unique among UK universities in offering a foundation year of interdisciplinary study before students decided on their major degree subject. In the end, history won out and I abandoned what I soon came to think of as the intellectual desert of modern languages.

The small number of contact hours suited me perfectly, allowing me to practise what I'd done for years: roam the library and find a convenient corner to work on my own. For the rest, there was the usual social intensity of undergraduate life on a residential campus, which for many meant embarking on a permanent cat-and-mouse game of trying to circumvent the (draconian and foolish) rules about visiting hours for the opposite sex. For a pioneering university, the place had an unhealthy obsession with the sex lives of its students. Those caught breaking the rules incurred unbelievably severe punishments: some shameful treatment was meted out, particularly to women. But young hormones normally found a way round even the most restrictive of conditions. Bizarre routines were played out, especially at weekends, that were worthy of a Whitehall farce, between young lovers and the university authorities. When the new sexually liberal spirit of the 1960s finally took hold – that Philip Larkin moment – the university paid for its foolishness by some terrible (but richly deserved) publicity. It was a fitting reward for the authorities' prurient curiosity about the private lives of young adults.

All this was far removed from home life and, inevitably perhaps, I began to drift away from my old life. It wasn't a deliberate or conscious rejection, and I didn't set out to distance myself from home. But that's what happened. It was also hastened by the family's relocation to the pub, which meant that home wasn't really home anymore. In any case I quickly developed a dislike for the new arrangements. It was clear that I would be better off – and certainly much happier – elsewhere. The problem wasn't Failsworth: it was family, or rather the new family that I no longer felt part of. Mum seemed happy enough, but whenever I went home within hours I felt the brittle disapproval of her new husband. He didn't seem to like me much, was always keen to catch me out on trivial issues, and quick to disagree or object to whatever I said. He was clearly distrustful of my life in general. 'I know you students. It's all sex and pills.' My answer, 'If only', was not designed to change his mind.

Though I made an effort to return periodically, I didn't linger, and the outcome was predictable. Vacations meant travel – to other parts of Britain and, in summers, as far away as possible, across Europe, to the Middle East and, of course, to France.

I had one final and furious session of disposing of the remaining items I'd left behind, but which I couldn't take to university. In a destructive outburst of about two hours, I destroyed and dumped all my old Sunday School prizes and those of my father before me. It was as if I'd torn up the past. Today the loss of those books remains a matter of deep regret, but perhaps I needed a clean break with the past. I wasn't prepared to leave behind what I couldn't take with me, so – out with the old.

What was I trying to break away from? With one exception, it certainly wasn't the people. I made dutiful visits to see those friends and relatives who mattered most, but even those visits became more infrequent. I was simply drifting away from everyone. Almost as an alternative, I became an inveterate writer of postcards and I had a list of people to whom I sent cards, normally within the first days of arriving somewhere new. Months later, when I turned up to visit people, I would see my last card still there, propped up on the mantelpiece.

I felt a deep attachment to Joe, and he remained a priority although I saw him less and less. Joe had been well and truly left on his own. His long-time lover had married someone else, his son was in the dubious care of another man, and

I had simply disappeared from view. All the people who had, for years, been part of his household arrangements had vanished, leaving him with the rudiments of a simple life: his work, his failing mother, and those evenings with his cigarettes in front of the fire.

There was to be a happy ending, however. At the age of 15, Ian finally broke away from home and moved in with a couple across the street from Joe. In the process, he spent a great deal of time with Joe and cared for him towards the end of his life. It was a final happy period for Joe, enjoying the company and affection of a son who had effectively been snatched away from him.

★ ★ ★

The one person I felt especially committed to was my widowed grandmother, and I made sure I visited her even when I saw no one else. I found her grubby old house strangely irresistible: her quirky absent-minded style, her genuine delight when I walked through the door, and her lavish farewells (an elaborate waving of both flabby white arms like a little fat windmill) as she stood at the door, until the last distant sight of me disappeared round the far corner of the street. She remained, to the end, Mrs Malaprop. On one of her 80th birthday celebrations she announced 'Your Uncle Harry sent some lovely flowers though Interpol'. (We celebrated that birthday twice, the first time when she was 78. She'd got the years wrong, and we simply believed her. Later, we couldn't decide whether it was a genuine mistake or yet another one of her infamous whoppers.)

She couldn't quite work out why, some years later, I started visiting Jamaica. She was aware that most people there were black, but apart from that she was in complete confusion. As I was leaving one summer for Jamaica she shouted to her nosey-parker next-door neighbour: 'Nelly! He's off to Nairobi!' She never failed. Grubby, loving and innocently confused to the end.

Our grandparents were simple working people who had lived out their lives in the starkest of circumstances. Grandpa, a physically tough little man, was breezily at ease with the world at large. He constantly struck up conversations with total strangers in the street. And all this despite the many worries heaped on him in the form of debts and the misdemeanours of various relatives. He took life's unexpected blows in his stride, and simply got on with things with his characteristic doggedness. Like his wife, he was uneducated and untutored, compassionate and loyal, often to people who did not deserve it.

As Alan and I grew older we both came to realise how lucky we had been, in the midst of our childhood poverty, to have had them as grandparents, not so much for their material and practical help (even though that had been invaluable) but for the unqualified affection they gave us. I don't pretend to know the deep psychological nature of this, but I do know that they provided a security and strength without which we might have been lost.

★ ★ ★

I was really pleased to be at university, but was slow to recognise how much it also meant to lots of my relatives and friends. Among the small inner circle of friends and relatives – the people who had been our safety net for years – there was genuine delight that an opportunity had come my way which none of them could remotely have dreamed about. Today, in an age of mass higher education, all this may seem odd. It didn't in 1960. Within days of settling in as students, it dawned on many of my new friends that we really *were* the lucky ones. Not only were most of us the first in our families to have broken into higher education, but we were the beneficiaries of a remarkable, and remarkably generous, state system. We had missed the nightmares of our parents' generation, had grown up under the protective shelter of the new welfare system, and were now enjoying free higher education. A short time before he died, when he knew I was heading to university, Grandpa Wood had put his finger on it, in his classically blunt style: 'You're a lucky bugger'. Hard to argue with that.